Like Me

Like Me

*Confessions of
a Heartland Country Singer*

Chely Wright

 Pantheon Books · New York

Pantheon Books and colophon are registered trademarks of Random House, Inc.

Grateful acknowledgment is made to Hal Leonard Corporation for permission
to reprint an excerpt from "Love in the Hot Afternoon," words and music
by Vince Matthews and Kent Westberry, copyright © 1970 by Universal—
Songs of Polygram International, Inc. Copyright renewed. All rights reserved.
Reprinted by permission of Hal Leonard Corporation.

Library of Congress Cataloging-in-Publication Data
Wright, Chely, [date].
Like me : confessions of a heartland country singer / Chely Wright.
        p.   cm.
ISBN 978-0-307-37886-6
1. Wright, Chely, 1970–.   2. Country musicians—United States—
Biography.   3. Singers—United States—Biography.   4. Lesbian musicians—
United States—Biography.   I. Title.
ML420.W75A3   2010
782.421642092—dc22
        [B]   2009043483

www.pantheonbooks.com

Printed in the United States of America

First Edition

1 3 5 7 9 10 8 6 4 2

For my family

History will have to record that the greatest tragedy of this period of social transition was not the strident clamor of the bad people, but the appalling silence of the good people.

—MARTIN LUTHER KING, JR.

Contents

Preface

It has been twenty-eight days since she last spoke to me. How can she not call or reach out in some way? I have no idea if I'm going crazy or if I'm already there. Is this what it feels like?

I went to the doctor to get a checkup. Dr. Hock said I weigh 109 pounds. Last time I weighed myself, I was at 120. I have no appetite. I wake up crying, I go to sleep crying. I walk around my house in the middle of the night, from room to room, trying to find something to distract me, something to stimulate me, something to keep me from breaking down.

I'm afraid of the thoughts that I'm having. My only relief is when I'm sleeping. Sleep, however, is elusive. It mocks me, it teases me, it tortures me. When I am able to get rest, I risk dreaming of her. The dreams are happy ones, but then I wake and feel the truth bearing down on me, forcing the air out of my lungs, leaving just enough for me to cry. It's like when I was a kid and got the wind knocked out of me and had to struggle to gasp the words "I can't breathe." I lie there hoping that I'm in a dream inside of a dream and that I will wake up.

I wonder if this is how it feels for everyone who is as broken as I am. I always assumed that people who committed suicide were somehow weak. Now I know how pain can seep into every cell of your body, and how hopelessness can shatter rationale and reason. Later, when I try to explain my despair, I will be asked, "Did you really love her that much? Was losing her bad enough to make you want to die?" My answer will be no, but while I was going through it, I was certain it would destroy me.

On the twenty-eighth day after the breakup, my eyes slowly opened, beating the sunrise by fifteen minutes. I lay in bed, feeling every fiber of my muscles, the nerves behind my eyes, and every square inch of skin on my bony frame. Everything hurt. I'd been in my pajamas since New Year's Day, except for a red-carpet event in downtown Nashville. "I'm going to come get you and carry you down the red carpet if I have to," ordered my beloved friend and tour manager, Jan. "You're going to get up, take a shower, do your hair and makeup, put on a dress, okay?" I didn't have the strength to argue, and since Jan didn't know about my secret or my broken heart, I gave in.

I noticed a vertical crease between my eyes that hadn't been there before. At first, it appeared only when I cried, but I'd spent so much time crying that it had become permanent. Outside, it was so freezing cold that I kept to the third floor of my house, because it was a few degrees warmer up there. My grand piano was downstairs. If I could, I would have pulled it into bed with me. Instead, I picked up my Gibson J-200. I didn't know how to play the guitar beyond a few chords, but songs were coming to me—pouring out of me, in fact. Most days I played until my fingers bled. I was convinced that the guitar and those songs were keeping me alive. When I'd finish a song, get it just right, do a simple recording of it in my home studio, another melody or phrase would scratch at the back of my throat or try to force itself out of the tips of my raw fingers. I needed a break, but I kept writing.

Two weeks into the breakdown, I stopped trying to fight off my anger. I couldn't defend her to myself anymore. She'd cry to me, saying she didn't know how she could fit us into her life. She promised she'd try, because she'd never loved anyone the way that she loved me. She asked me to hang in there with her. Then she'd run away. I gave in to my frustrations with her and began to steep in my anger at the way society forces people like us into such dark places. And in the wee hours of an achingly cold day in the first month of 2006, I'd never been in a darker place.

I'd been in hiding most of my life and worked hard to protect my secret. No one like me in country music has ever admitted his or her homosexuality. There are gays in Nashville, but as far as anyone is led to believe, they are not those of us on the magazine covers. There is a slight understanding that there are gay publicists, songwriters, hair and makeup artists in the country music industry who help sell "straight" stars to the public, but that's it. And even among them, few are truly out of the closet.

I was a successful recording artist, a video star. I'd made *People* magazine's 50 Most Beautiful People list. Men in the armed forces asked me to autograph their Chely Wright posters. I'd been seen around town with a host of famous men—Brad Paisley, Vince Gill, Troy Aikman, and Brett Favre.

How could I be gay? Well, I am.

I reflect on a life that seems to be filled with all-American accomplishment. I was class president and homecoming queen in my senior year of high school. The Academy of Country Music's Top New Female Vocalist. The first entertainer to play for our troops in Iraq after the fall of Saddam Hussein. I was the American Legion's Woman of the Year and my home state's Kansan of the Year. I founded Reading, Writing & Rhythm, a charity that has raised more than a million dollars for public schools. I am known to country music fans around the world as the singer of the #1 hit "Single White Female."

On that morning, I realized my secret had caught up with me. I might be able to hide from Nashville and my fans, but I could no longer hide from myself. Even if I had been able to fight my way out of this emotional abyss, I'd still be lying. Lying had already cost me a twelve-year relationship with Julia, the person with whom I once hoped to spend the rest of my life. Now it had claimed my relationship with Kristin, the woman with whom I'd just broken up. Denial and fear forced us apart. Denial and fear told Kristin it was better to hide than choose what her heart wanted. But I was no better. Behind closed doors I couldn't be the real me. So on the twenty-sixth day of 2006, I decided it would be better to stop fighting.

I went upstairs to my bedroom, got on a stepladder, and reached up high into my closet. I easily located the loaded 9 mm handgun. It was heavier than I remembered. I stared at it for a few seconds, then made my way with the weapon down three flights of stairs to my first-floor foyer. The gun felt so strange in my hand. I didn't hold it tightly; I carried it as if it were a dirty diaper or a piece of rotten food. I held it out and away. It made a clunking noise as I set it on the mantel of my entryway fireplace. I stood there, staring at it. I remember wondering how people do it. Do they put it to their temple and pull the trigger? Do they put it in their mouth? That made more sense to me; I didn't want to miss. If I pointed it into my mouth, I probably wouldn't miss.

I said a prayer to God to forgive me and to understand why I couldn't go on anymore like this. I begged God to realize that I would never be able to fit into the life that I'd created. I hoped that God would realize that I would never be accepted.

I picked up the gun and put the end of it in my mouth. It was cold. I held it steady and got my right thumb on the trigger and prepared to pull it by pushing it outward. I looked up into the mirror, the one built into the mantel. I struggle now to fully explain what I saw staring back at me. My mouth stretched open with the end of a gun in it . . . My eyes were wide open, bigger than they'd ever been. It occurred to me that I wasn't crying. Don't people cry when they kill themselves? I recall thinking, "What if I do this and somehow my eyes stay open and whoever discovers me here sees my eyes like that?" So I closed my eyes . . . thumb still on the trigger. My mind went a million miles a minute. I thought of my family, my dogs, my friends, my fans, the sun, a kiss from Julia, and music. Then I heard a noise.

It was the sound of my heart, pounding in my head. It grew louder and louder and I just knew that something was about to happen. I couldn't stand here in my foyer with my eyes closed and a gun in my mouth forever. Then it happened—I started to cry. I opened my eyes and looked in that mirror as the tears poured out. I took the gun out of my mouth, put it back up on the mantel, and headed up to the third floor. I climbed in bed and stayed there for the next two days.

Like Me

The Prayer

Dear God, please don't let me be gay. I promise to
be a good person. I promise not to lie. I promise not
to steal. I promise to always believe in you. I promise to do all the things you ask me to do. Please take
it away. In your name I pray. Amen.

I said this prayer every single day of my life since the third
grade. The words changed over the years, but the sentiment
remained the same. The prayer was as much a part of me as
my brown eyes, my long toes, and the chicken pox scar in the
middle of my forehead.

I don't remember a time when I didn't believe in God. And I
hardly remember a time when I didn't know I was different.
Slowly, I would learn that difference was something to be hated
and feared. For most of my thirty-nine years, I've hidden my sexuality because I thought I had to. I was a small-town girl with a
dream of moving to Nashville and becoming a famous country
singer. The dream came true. But for all my success, I was left
wrestling with a secret that could destroy everything I'd built.
For decades, I swore I'd take that secret to my grave. Even as I
write this, only a handful of people beyond my family and closest
friends know that I am gay. But I'm done with hiding. I'm a
proud Kansan, a loving daughter, sister, and friend, a child of
God, and a lesbian. I was raised to know the difference between
right and wrong. Telling my story is the right thing to do.

My values were nurtured by my hometown of Wellsville, a
farming community of sixteen hundred tucked into the northeast corner of Franklin County, Kansas. Our main street was
called Main Street, and most drivers treated its single flashing

red stoplight as a mere suggestion to slow down. Although Kansas City was only about an hour away, we seldom left the city limits of Wellsville. Even after all this time, it's hard for me to find a stranger in the community of my younger years. Most folks know each other by name, schedule their social lives around high school football games, and spend Sundays at one of the two poles of spiritual life in town: the Baptist church and the Methodist church, which sit just fifty yards apart. Wellsville folks tend to marry their high school sweethearts and settle down to raise kids where they were brought up, just like their parents before them. It's the heart of the heartland, and I'm proud to call it home.

I'm the baby of three. We were each born a year apart, starting in the summer of 1967, when my mother, Cheri, was just nineteen. Some say I get my hardheadedness from my mom. When she was four, she was stricken with polio, and doctors said she'd be unable to walk, let alone bear children. From the time she contracted polio until she was nine years old, she spent most of her life in a hospital enduring surgeries that left her with a badly scarred right leg half the size of her left. But by junior high school, she'd set her mind on walking and tossed her crutches aside. Teased for her severe limp and the surgical scars that crisscrossed her legs, my mother simply got tougher. After she married my father, she was determined to have her babies without drugs or surgery. And she did.

At twenty-one, my father, Stan L. Wright, was barely a man himself when my older brother, Chris, arrived. When my dad was five years old, his father died suddenly of a ruptured appendix, leaving my grandmother to struggle to make ends meet. The only father figures he had known were a succession of husbands and boyfriends, most of whom never seemed to stick around long. When he was seventeen, my dad enlisted in the navy, but after he married my mother, he found jobs pouring concrete and working construction. Dad worked hard to support his growing family, but in many ways he wasn't ready for what comes with being a husband and parent. Luckily, my older brother was a stoic and self-sufficient kid almost from the beginning—or so goes the family lore. Good thing, because my sister, Jeny, came along only eleven months later.

I arrived late, in the fall of 1970, my mother's biggest baby at nine and a half pounds. I had long black hair that never fell out, fingernails grown out so far they curled down at the ends and—as my siblings love to point out—a soft coat of light hair down my back (thankfully, that pelt fell out). From the start, Jeny doted on me, trailing behind Mom while she cared for her newest baby. One of my earliest memories is seeing my big sister pushing her face through the bars of my crib, waiting for me to need something.

In the early years of my life, my parents scraped together enough money to buy a rickety white Victorian at 710 South Main Street that we all still call the Old House. At the turn of the century, the house had been called the Wayside Inn and was a boardinghouse for railroaders. I loved every rambling inch of it.

My father was a tenderhearted man, but he dealt with a life of hard knocks by drinking too much. When he drank, he could get mean, and it was always directed toward my mom. When I was three, Mom made an escape with the three of us kids in the middle of the night. With help from her sister, my aunt Char, she found a little pink house in the town of Ottawa and got a job at a twenty-four-hour dry cleaning store. Eventually, she agreed to take my dad back under one condition: he had to promise to stop drinking. Dad tried to make good on the deal, but occasionally he'd slip. There were times when he would go out coon hunting for the night and not return home in the morning. I'd get worried he'd been hurt in a hunting accident, but Mom always knew where he was. "Probably passed out drunk in his pickup," she'd say with an edge of bitterness in her voice. When he'd finally stumble in, she did seem happy and relieved that he

The Wright family, portrait taken at the Nebraska State Fair. 1973.

was just drunk . . . and not dead. The tension between my parents hung over all of us. They argued about everything, and in our hearts my siblings and I knew they'd be better off apart. Still, whatever troubled their marriage, we knew they loved us.

In many ways, my folks were visionaries. They were true entrepreneurs and could usually create a plan and execute it well. Of course, I believe a secret to many of their successful endeavors was that they had a built-in workforce of three strong kids who did exactly what we were told to do. My brother, my sister, and I were not spared real, manual, hard labor during our growing-up years. Some of it we dreaded; some of it was incredibly fun.

When those winter months would clamp down on rural Kansas, it was not out of the ordinary for the mercury to drop below zero for weeks on end or for twenty inches of snow to fall in a day's time. My dad and the three of us kids would bundle up in layers of thermals, jeans, overalls, and coveralls and head out to the timber to cut firewood. Kansas kids love snow and we were always excited to go out in it, whether it be for fun or for work. Sometimes my mother, even though she was handicapped, would go along and do what she could to help. She was tough, and my folks taught all of us how to work hard and how to do a good job.

We'd park the pickup truck as far into the woods as possible, then carry the axes and chain saws the rest of the way in to the trees that we'd be taking down that day. My dad was the only one strong enough to run the big chain saw at the time, so we stood back and tried to figure out where not to be when the tree came down. Once it was toppled, we got to work. We cut the smaller branches off with our little saws, then rolled and tipped the big logs up on end so they could be ripped in half with an axe. Those pieces of wood were split smaller and smaller until they were all of a similar size that could easily fit into a stove or fireplace in someone's home. We used our little human assembly line to move our big stack of hickory through the woods. Jeny and I would usually be singing some country music song at the top of our lungs. We sang and we worked. We'd load the wood into perfect rows in the back of the truck, making use of every square inch. We wanted to be able to get it all in the truck as neatly as we could to cut down on the number of times we had to load the truck. Then we would drive to our destination, unload it, stack it again, and get paid for it. On those cold winter days, we'd do this from the time the sun came up until long after the sun went down. I don't know how much my dad charged the people we delivered wood to, but it must've been enough to get us by.

When we got back to the house, Mom would have us pry ourselves out of our wet, frozen clothes and she'd serve us each a big bowl of her chili or her ham 'n beans. I don't recall my folks ever saying a special "thank you" to us kids for our hard work, but there was a general sense of "way to go, guys . . . you did good" in the air. I lived for that feeling.

My parents taught us that if we were willing to work, we could make it anywhere.

I had a paper route in first grade, and six days a week I threw the *Lawrence Daily Journal World*. In addition to our paying jobs, we had household and farm chores for which we were fully responsible. We didn't have a nice home, but it was spotless. We didn't have flowers in the yard, but the grass was always freshly cut. We didn't have nice clothes, but they were clean.

When I was six, I asked my mom if I could be baptized. "I think you might be too young, Squirrelly," said my mom. She sat down at the kitchen table that my dad had made with leftover lumber, lit up a Viceroy, and told me to sit. She asked me to explain to her what it would mean to be baptized. We talked about as long as that cigarette lasted, then she smashed it out in a Kansas City Chiefs ashtray. She stood up, and as she headed to the utility room in the back of the house she said, "Well, you better go see Warren and see what he says."

Warren Skiles was the preacher of the Wellsville Community Baptist Church, a congregation we stuck with for a few years. He lived three houses down with his wife, Connie. I took off running and found him in his side yard, tending to his honeybees. He could see I meant business, and he carefully latched the little white wooden box where he kept his hive, taking me up to his front porch to talk.

I spoke in a great breathless wave: "I want to be baptized but Mom said I might not be old enough because she says that you have to understand what it means to invite Jesus into your heart and that He will be your Lord and Savior, but I DO know what it means and even though I'm only six, I really DO think that I'm ready to be baptized but Mom says that I have to talk to you first because you're the one who decides. What do you think, Warren?" Warren responded by taking me in his arms, laughing, and shouting "Hallelujah." Then we sat a while on his front porch, sipping Connie's iced tea, and talked about God and the world.

I was baptized the next Sunday.

My mother talked a lot about faith, and I really believe that she was genuine in hers. She read the Bible somewhat regularly and taught me to turn to the Bible for answers about any questions that I might have in life. She wasn't one to quote scripture, but she seemed to have a clear understanding of the stories in the Bible and what they meant to her. I have always considered her to be what I call a blue-collar Christian. She'd told me that God was so powerful and great that if I ever did have a question or problem for God to help me with, I could turn to the Bible even if I didn't know where to look. She showed me how to hold the Bible, say a prayer for enlightenment, and then randomly open the book and start to read. She told me that there was no way to go wrong, that God would always reveal the answer or some guidance in the pages. At times, I felt that this ritual helped me find answers and direction that I needed, but it could've been that I felt better simply because I allowed myself to be submissive to God. It's not a big issue to me to know the root of why my relationship with God works . . . it just does. And for that I'm thankful.

I felt torn between the teachings of the handful of churches that I'd attended in my short life. Each church said things a little differently, but they all seemed to be reading from the same Bible. I wondered how that could be. This made me contemplate that one could interpret the exact same scripture different ways. I made note that even in my small town, people believed in different things—so much so that they went to a specific church.

Me at age six. 1976.

If they didn't, and if God's word was so clear and so easily understood, they'd all go to the same church. If little Wellsville, Kansas, could have so much religious diversity and conflict, the rest of the world was probably at religious odds too.

Jeny and I had been regularly attending the Wellsville Assembly of God Church when we were around the ages of twelve and eleven, respectively. My mom had informed us months before that our family was no longer members of whatever church it was that we'd attended for a year or so. So Jeny and I sought out a new church. We didn't have a long list of criteria that determined which one to try. We had just two, actually. It needed to be a church that we hadn't already belonged to, of course, and the other criterion was that Jeny and I would have to be able to make the journey on our bikes. I knew the preacher and his wife of the Assembly of God church because I was their papergirl, and they invited me to come to see their church.

My sister and I were instantly welcomed by the congregation, and since the town was so small, we already knew the faces and most of the names of the people who worshiped there. I remember one Sunday service at that church in particular, when a few people started shouting out words that I didn't understand. I looked at Jeny to see if she was as confused as I was, and she was. An elder of the congregation came to the pew where I was seated and grabbed my hand. He pulled me out of the row and led me into the aisle. I resisted and tried to sit back down. He said a few things really loudly to me while putting his palm on the very top of my head. I recall that he pushed down so hard on my head that he pressed one of my hair barrettes into my scalp. He then said, in plain English words that I understood, that I should go ahead and do it. I had no idea what he was talking about, so I just shrugged my shoulders. He told me that I too had the gift of speaking in tongues and that I should go ahead and speak it . . . to show everyone the "blessed gift that God has given you." I said nothing. I didn't know what to do, and I certainly didn't have any special words to say. I didn't feel disappointed that God didn't love me enough to give me "the gift," but I did feel scared that the elder who had grabbed my hand had some kind of spooky power. That frightened me. I wondered if he had another special gift that could tell him that I got crushes on girls instead of boys. Jeny and I never returned to that church.

I have always felt lucky that my list of reasons for hiding my homosexuality most of my life didn't include "God disapproves of gays." Not one church or religion to which I was exposed had anything other than condemnation for homosexuality, but somehow I didn't fully buy it. I did fear that God would disapprove of my feelings of homosexuality during my childhood, but fear of God never lingered in my heart for long. I felt that God's love for me was powerful and unshakable. I know what I've heard religious people say about the Bible—that it specifically says homosexuality is wrong. I have read those parts of the Bible too, and by and large, the Bible is tricky to read, difficult to comprehend, and impossible to apply to modern times. I can tell you this much: even if the Bible were to read, "Chely Wright . . . if you're reading this, be clear that it is a sin for you to love another female and for you to desire to partner with her for life," I'd find it unsettling, but I would still know that this is who I am, exactly how God created me and that His love for me is infinite.

I did feel love in the years to come, from my family and from the close knit small town that nurtured my success as a singer. But most of the time I felt fear. I was afraid that people would discover I was different, so I made it my mission to be good at everything else. I was scared that I was a failure already, because I was gay. But I did everything I could to make up for that fundamental flaw.

When I was nine years old, on New Year's Eve, the Old House burned to the ground. My whole family stood shivering in the twelve-degree weather in the dead of night, watching the volunteer fire department struggle to contain the blaze. They turned every hose they had on that white clapboard structure, but every time water hit wood, it bounced right off in little beads of ice. We never learned what caused the inferno that consumed the Old House, but all these years later I still dream of 710 South Main.

At the time, I had a good idea of what caused the fire; I thought it was because of me. The ninth year of my life was scary for me, and the last day of that year was a fitting punctuation mark. After the Old House was ashes, life got much harder.

Learning to Hide

When people ask me when I knew I was attracted to women, I can only say that on some level I've always known. Before my first crush, I sensed I was different. But when I felt that attraction, I knew the difference was my homosexuality. Everything started to add up and it didn't look good.

A couple of weeks before the beginning of my third-grade year, Jeny and I sprinted down to the school, as we did every day in the final days of summer vacation that led up to the first day of classes. There were usually three teachers for each grade, and our mission was to find out which teacher we'd be assigned to. When the school administration had made its decisions, a copy of names and teachers would be taped on the inside of a window just off of the elementary school office.

My name was underneath a teacher's name that I didn't recognize. Miss Smilie. I thought it was interesting that she was not a Mrs. or even a Ms., but a Miss. This whole Miss business confused me.

Miss Smilie was newly out of college and enthusiastic about being our teacher. She had the prettiest, whitest teeth I'd ever seen and her skin was golden brown. She didn't wear makeup, and she didn't need any. She wore bib overalls to school every

Miss Smilie's third-grade class. I'm front-row center. 1979.

day and I sensed that it became a problem with Mr. Peterson, our grade school principal. After months and months of the overalls, she stopped wearing them and started coming to class in a skirt. I asked her as we were walking in from recess one day why she didn't wear her overalls anymore, and she said she was told that teachers don't wear bib overalls to school and she needed to find something different to wear.

My brother, sister, and I loved school. Even if we were feeling sick, we would go to class. I'd arrive early when I could, just so I didn't miss anything. That year, I began dreading Fridays. I didn't like being away from school for the weekend. I realized that it wasn't so much the other students, the recess, the tasty lunch served every day, or the gratification of the learning process that I was longing for on the weekends. I was missing my teacher.

I would wonder throughout the day on Saturday and Sunday what she might be doing. I wondered who her friends were. I didn't think of her in terms of kissing and other kinds of physical contact, I just thought of her as someone that I wanted to be near. I believe that heterosexual third graders who might have a crush on someone of the opposite sex probably felt the same way I did. I doubt that a straight third-grade girl has fantasies about having sexual contact with a boy, but rather imagines simply being near him and getting his affection.

I paid close attention to the other little girls in my class, trying to determine if they felt like I did about Miss Smilie. I hoped that I would identify it in other girls. I prayed that it was perfectly normal to fall for my teacher, who was very much a woman. I saw no such signs in my female classmates. My stomach would feel uneasy and sick every time I thought about it. I knew that I was in a bad situation, and I was painfully aware that I had no one to talk to and nowhere to turn.

I don't even think I'd heard the word "homosexual" before or understood what it meant, but I'd certainly heard jokes that adults and high school kids would tell that included the words "faggot," "fairy," "dyke," and "queer" in them. When I heard people talking about faggots, dykes, fairies, and queers, I wondered what one looked like. We didn't have them in Wellsville, as far as I knew. I'd also heard some things in church that led me to know that certain words and activities were negative. I had heard the words "whore," "criminal," "drunk," "homosexual," "pervert," "liar," and "non-believer" all strung together so many times that I understood that those were the building blocks of sin and evildoing.

Friday nights were a pretty big deal when I was young because my parents allowed us to stay up as late as we wanted. After the ten o'clock news there was a program called *Friday Fright Night,* and we could usually count on two very scary movies to be aired back to back. Most nights, we'd fall asleep shortly after the second one began, but we loved our ceremony of popcorn, Pepsi, and scary movies.

One particular Friday night would cause me years of worry and unbelievable fear. My dad happened to decide to stay up with us to watch the double feature. Chris got tired during the first one and went to bed. Jeny fell asleep on the floor wrapped snugly in a quilt that my great-grandmother had sewn, probably years before any of us were born. That left my dad and me to watch the second movie alone. I'm sure I was tired, but I was bound and determined to show my dad how long I could stay awake.

The movie began to play. We watched the entire thing from start to finish, and I was petrified. Even though I needed to go to the bathroom halfway through the movie, I stayed snuggled on the couch next to my dad. The scenes of that movie, the story, and the sounds that came out of our console television on that night would stay with me and haunt me for days, weeks, months, and years to come.

I was convinced, after seeing it, that I was in danger of being possessed by the devil. The main character of the movie was an all-American little girl around my age whose body was inexplicably overtaken by Satan himself. I questioned my mom about it in the following days, and once she got over the complete shock that my father had allowed her youngest child at nine years old to watch *The Exorcist,* she explained her position on the devil and how unlikely it was that I'd be possessed by an evil spirit. She tried to convince me that I was a good kid, even if I sometimes got in trouble. She told me I was a normal kid like everyone else and that the devil didn't go after normal kids to do his dirty work. Well, that's all she needed to say for me to know that I was in deep spiritual trouble. I was not normal. I was the opposite of normal. Everything around me, whether it was overt language, subtle suggestion, or non-spoken actions, told me that there was something unacceptable about me.

I continued to love Miss Smilie, even though I didn't want to. I put myself through little emotional and behavioral obstacle courses, willing myself to resist the urge to like her. I'd try to go the whole day in class without looking at her. My feelings for her were sinful, I believed, so I did my best to avoid my feelings. My stomach continued to hurt, and I was so hopeful after third grade passed that being away from Miss Smilie would fix me.

The next year I developed a new crush. My mom's cousin Sam Finnell and his family lived in Leavenworth, Kansas, just a couple of hours by car from Wellsville. Sam and MaryAnn Finnell had three daughters. Marcia was two years older than my brother, Tracey was my sister's age, and Sammie Sue just a few months younger than me. Mom's cousin Sam was an amazing piano player and I idolized him for that. Sam and his family were good, kind, and funny people. We played music, played cards, battled at board games, went camping with them and their beloved dachshund, and shared a million laughs. They were the fun relatives that we didn't get to see that often, but when we did, we had a ball.

Since Sammie Sue and I were close in age, I usually spent my time with her when our families got together. She was obsessed with Rod Stewart and was convinced that she was his long-lost love child. She had her hair cut like his and dressed like him.

I loved playing with Sammie Sue, but I found myself inventing reasons to go upstairs where Marcia's room was to have the chance to walk past her door and try to peek in. She was nice to me, and the Finnell sisters actually got along well with one another. So when I'd suggest to Sammie Sue or Tracey and Jeny that we go up to Marcia's room and ask her if she wanted to play Monopoly, they were always agreeable. Most of the time Marcia would stop what she was doing, which was usually talking on the phone to her boyfriend, and play with us. All of Sam and Mary-Ann's daughters were beautiful, and Marcia was no exception.

A short time after one of our weekend visits up to the Finnells' home, my mom received a piece of mail from MaryAnn. I brought it in from the mailbox that sat atop a post poked in the ground at the end of our gravel driveway and announced excitedly to my mom that we got something from the Finnells. She opened it, read the little handwritten note, and pulled three wallet-sized school pictures of the Finnell girls from the white envelope. My mom got up from the kitchen table, walked over to the refrigerator, and secured each little photo to the freezer door with three separate magnets, each slightly resembling a different type of colorful fruit. I walked over and studied the pictures. Sammie Sue had her blond hair spiked way up high just like her fantasy father, Rod Stewart. Tracey looked pretty, and it occurred to me then how much I thought she and my sister looked alike. Then I took a long look at Marcia's picture. She was the prettiest of them all, I thought. I felt blood rushing to my cheeks and to my arms and legs. My tummy did a flip with a double twist. That was the first time that my body felt any kind of sexual excitement that I could remember.

For a few days, that fridge was like a drug. I couldn't resist the force that made me want to go near it. I'd find a reason to go into the kitchen and I'd casually walk by her picture, most of the time not daring to stop and stare, but just slowing my steps ever so slightly. I'd pause just enough to focus on her, tipping my chin to the floor to throw off anyone who might see me but cutting my eyes upward to look at beautiful Marcia Finnell. After a few days of doing this, I was so scared of getting caught that I decided it was time to move to Plan B: I stole the picture.

In a purposeful and planned tactical maneuver, I walked right by our almond-colored Kenmore and swiped the two-by-three-inch photo. I went directly to the bathroom in the hallway. It was the only safe place to be, because I could lock the door once I got in there. I locked the door, slid down the paneled wall onto the floor, and looked at that picture for what seemed to be an eternity. It was time for me to hide Marcia's picture in that bathroom. Underneath the sink was a cabinet where my mom would put Comet, Pine-Sol, a box of hair curlers, and stacks of toilet paper. Inside that cabinet, on the underneath side of the countertop, there were a couple of support boards that held the sink up flush with the counter. That's where I hid the picture. No one would ever reach up there for any reason. I gave the picture one more look, kissed it, and put it in its safe hiding place. Marcia Finnell was my crush in fourth grade and as much as I loved her, I was learning to hate myself.

I continued to pay close attention to others around me in hopes that I might be able to find someone else like me, but I saw no signs that would lead me to believe that I wasn't alone. Being a homosexual was not a phase, as I'd hoped it would be.

If there were other girls in Wellsville like me, I didn't know how to find them. I knew of no books in my school library or our little city library that addressed homosexuality. If they existed, I never would have dared check them out anyway, for fear of someone noticing.

I was a tomboy who liked to go hunting with my dad and play quarterback in tackle football games with my brother and his friends. Chris would always suggest that I be the cheerleader, but when push came to shove, he'd give in because he knew I was just as good as the boys. I recall one time in the front yard of the Old House when some of his friends had come over for a game, and one of the boys cried out, "Oh, no, we're not letting a girl play!" Chris replied, "My sister's playing with us—she's way better than you anyway."

But I also liked dresses and dolls. Other than the fact that Jeny and I would cut our dolls' hair with pinking shears and paint their eyelids with fingernail polish, we cared for our babies as if they were live humans.

"House of the Rising Sun"

Loretta, Buck Owens, Tammy Wynette—those Nashville legends were like members of my family. We didn't have money, but we always had music in our home. My folks declared that our family identity was Country, just as some people identify themselves as Democrats or Republicans. Because of that, I grew up thinking all the music played in our house—including the Beatles, Chuck Berry, and Elvis—had to be country music.

I loved it when my dad would strum his twelve-string acoustic or his Gibson J-45. Like most members of my family, he was self-taught, but he was one of the steadiest rhythm guitar players around. Mom sang and kept a three-ring binder full of handwritten lyrics to her favorite songs that she'd had longer than she'd had me. While she took the melody, Dad would sing on the choruses and try to do a little harmony. I'd join in to help him out, and he'd smile and say, "That sounds good, Squirrelly!" I could also sense my mom's pride in my singing ability. I don't think my folks were ever happier than at times like those, and neither was I.

On Saturday nights at our house, we'd often have a pickin' party. A dozen people would cram into the TV room singing Hank Williams, Sr., and Tom T. Hall, the cigarette smoke hanging above them like a cloud. I was the only kid interested in being where the adults and the music were. I hated the smoke, but I was drawn to the songs and camaraderie in that room. I started playing piano at four years old—lessons were an extravagance my parents somehow managed to pay for—and I loved it when the grown-ups would invite me to take part in those jam sessions. The first time I had the chance to sing a solo, I was around six, and I belted out the tune "House of the Rising Sun." I have no idea why I settled on the 1964 pop hit by the Animals, but my dad played it on guitar and I thought it would sound good to play the piano along with him while I sang. I walked over to the Henry F. Miller console piano that sat against the wall, opened it up, and wailed out the blues classic about a lost soul abandoned in a New Orleans brothel.

When it came to the piano, my fingers just seemed to know where to go. At the time I sang "House of the Rising Sun," most of the songs that I knew had three chords, sometimes four, but that tune has five or six. The progression started out in a minor chord and that would set the musical tone for the entire song. I loved how dramatic those chords felt, and I was proud that I needed all ten of my fingers to play the arrangement that I'd constructed. I gave myself over to the lyrics and relished how good the words felt in my throat, letting the somber melody float on top of those beautiful chords. It makes me laugh when I remember myself as a Kansas farm girl singing the blues to a room full of my elders. Still, I sang with total conviction. I already knew being a singer was my destiny.

Bullies

I loved pencils, Big Chief paper, new Crayolas, and school lunch. Before I was old enough to start kindergarten, I'd get up in the mornings with Chris and Jeny and follow them around the house as they prepared for their days of scholastic adventure. I wanted to go to school so badly, and it was torture for me to be left behind. I persuaded my mom to help me stay up to speed with them, so she'd spend time with me each day on schoolwork. I was able to read and write before I started kindergarten, and I think that's one of the reasons I went on to do well in school.

My pursuit of being a model pupil went smoothly for me until fourth grade. My teacher was Mrs. Lawyer and I was not only her student but her papergirl as well. That was the year I learned that some people are just plain mean.

There was a girl in my class that I was afraid of. It was better to be her friend than not. At the beginning of the school year, Jane had been my friend.

There was another girl in our class named Cecilia. She had always had a rough time in school, and fourth grade may have been the zenith of her misery. For some reason, Jane locked in on Cecilia and did her best to make her life hell. Jane took a small plastic box that held each student's lunch ticket out of Mrs. Lawyer's desk and kept it until Mrs. Lawyer noticed that it was missing. Once Mrs. Lawyer realized that the box was missing, she questioned the class; no one seemed to know anything about it. A couple of lunch-ticketless days went by, and it became a big deal in our grade school world. We'd all been interrogated, and at that point the issue became less about the box and more about the fact that someone had stolen it and was lying.

Then on the third day, during recess, Jane said to me, "Come on, come with me back to the classroom for a minute." She opened her desk and there was the box. I screamed out, "Oh, wow, you found it!" With a determined look on her face, she grabbed my hair, twisted it hard, and told me that I'd better shut my mouth. Then Jane took the box over to Cecilia's desk, lifted the top, and shoved it in. We went back to the playground, and I had to work hard to fight back the tears.

I have no idea how Jane got her information, but the minute we got back from recess, Mrs. Lawyer and another teacher informed us that our desks were to be searched immediately. They found what they were looking for in Cecilia's desk, and she was in big trouble.

I'm not certain how long I wrestled with what I knew, but it was eating me alive. I kept trying to get up the nerve to tell on Jane, who was a charismatic leader and could get most anyone to do anything, while convincing them to abandon all judgment and fear of consequences.

I asked Mrs. Lawyer one morning, right before the bell rang, if I could talk to her, and of course she said yes. At some point during the day she put down her chalk on the little metal shelf under the blackboard and said in front of the entire class, "Chely, I need to see you outside." In my head I was screaming, "What the heck did you do *that* for? Now Jane will know that I talked to you!" I got up, looked at Jane as if I had no idea why I was being called outside, and walked out the door.

We sat down on the concrete stoop of the building and Mrs. Lawyer said, "You said you needed to talk to me. What do you need to talk to me about?" I said, "Oh, I can't remember. I forgot." To which she sarcastically replied, "Oh, okay." We just sat there for what seemed to be an entire minute, in silence. I asked her if I could go back in and she said, "Nope." Another few seconds went by, and I just buried my face in my hands and began to sob. She put her arm around my shoulder and asked me if something was wrong at home. I told her no. "Chely, you can tell me anything," she said, "and I will help you." I took a deep breath and like a volcano of truth, I erupted. I told her every detail of what Jane had done.

She said that I'd made a good decision in telling her and that it took a lot of courage to do it. I didn't feel courageous. I felt scared and sick to my stomach. I was so worked up after telling her that she sent me to the principal's office to lie down for a few minutes to get myself together before coming back to class. She must've played it super cool when she went back into the room, because I don't think Jane ever realized that it was I who told on her.

That Christmas, after the holiday break, Cecilia and I were both using the pencil sharpener that was barely clinging to the wall in the back of the classroom when I noticed she had on brand-new tennis shoes and some nice clothes I hadn't seen before. I told her I really liked her shoes and her pants and asked if she got them for Christmas. She cupped her hand up by my ear and whispered, "Mrs. Lawyer got them for me and two more pair of jeans, but don't tell anyone, okay?" I said I wouldn't.

Cecilia was a nice girl and probably would have been a good friend for me to have, but I was too afraid to buddy up with her because she was a target of Jane and her cronies. I knew that she had gotten a raw deal, and I recall thinking that Mrs. Lawyer was like a superhero, righting the wrongs of the universe. I hoped there was a chance that I'd grow up to be a person who did kind things for others.

I had some more difficult times in my last couple of years in elementary school. I was torn between not wanting anyone to notice me and wanting everyone to notice me. I wanted to be the first one up in front of the class for speeches and oral book reports and the first chosen as a teammate for a game of kickball. I lived for the times Mrs. Cramer, our grade school music teacher, let me play the piano and sing a song for everyone in music class, yet I was terrified of being identified as different. I was full of shame, and brimming with confidence all at the same time.

Those were the years that boys and girls started getting crushes and going steady. This was a problem for me. I tried as hard as I could to have a crush on a boy, but it just wasn't working. I could identify which ones were cute and which ones were cool. I wasn't stupid—I was just gay. I followed the rules and never got into trouble. That is, until fifth grade.

The girls were fighting with one another over who was getting the attention from the boys. And when a boy paid attention to me, I felt the resentment and jealousy from the other girls. If only they had known I wasn't interested. My main tormentors were a group of girls led by Jane, who would be my nemesis until the day I left Wellsville.

One day that winter, my entire class went to the school library to check out books. By then, cliques had formed, and I found myself on my own. I was standing by myself in an aisle of books, trying to choose one to take home. Without warning, a contraband snowball hit me like a bullet, right above the left eye. I looked up and saw the shooter: Danielle Green, surrounded by Jane and a gaggle of laughing girls. I will never forget the fury I felt. I lunged toward Danielle—she didn't even have time to run. I grabbed her with both hands by the throat and tackled her to the ground. I was sitting on her chest, throwing punches at her head and face.

The other kids had gathered around us, and I could hear Mrs. Allendar, the librarian, yelling at us to stop. I didn't stop, but as I was punching Danielle in the face, I remember telling myself not to hit her as hard as I could. I held back, not wanting to hurt her too much or make her bleed, but wanting those girls to see that I wasn't going to take it anymore. Mrs. Allendar pulled me off of Danielle just as I began to cry. I hated that I cried; it weakened what I wanted them to hear: that I was not a girl to be messed with.

We were both sent to the principal's office. Mr. Peterson sent me home with a note to my mom, who knew of the difficult time I was having with those girls. She and my dad held a pretty hard line on school and getting in trouble in school—it wasn't allowed. However, we kids were told that if we ever got into a fight at school, they better not find out that we'd thrown the first punch. Those were Stan and Cheri's rules of engagement. This time, I was able to make my parents understand that the snowball was technically the first punch.

My mom handwrote a response on the back of the note that was sent home with me, and I delivered it to my fifth-grade teacher. It said something to the effect of "I read the note and Chely told me what happened. If she was hit in the face with a snowball first, then I'm fine with her hitting Danielle Green. Thank you, Cheri Wright."

My teacher, Mrs. Raugewitz, read the note and sent me to the office to give it to Mr. Peterson. He read it, sent me back to class, and that was the end of it.

I don't even think the snowball left a bruise above my eye, but I felt battered. In sixth grade, the bullying continued. That year I started thinking that if I had the right clothes, I might fit in better. I wanted Jordache jeans and Nike tennis shoes so badly, but our family didn't have enough money to get designer jeans or name-brand tennis shoes; our new clothes typically came from the JCPenney outlet store in Kansas City. Their inventory was

I was eleven years old and filled with fear that there was something really wrong with me. At that time, I was convinced I was in big trouble with God. As I look at this picture now, I can see the burden in my eyes.

factory seconds—pants with crooked seams and pockets sewn on unevenly, sweaters with holes in them. It was embarrassing, but it was the most my family could afford. Maybe if I'd had those Nike tennis shoes, I thought, sixth grade wouldn't have turned out to be such a disaster.

When the popular girls did let me into their circle, I couldn't enjoy it. When they needed my book smarts or a solid softball or basketball player, I was included. And if they needed a well-spoken model student to make a plea on behalf of my peers to an adult, I was the chosen one. They recognized my strengths, but they also knew my weaknesses: I was sensitive, I was scared, and I was poor.

The playground for the Wellsville Elementary School was directly behind our classroom, and that year a huge new wooden jungle gym was being built right before our eyes. It was to be a couple of stories high, consisting of walkways, ropes, poles, chains, ladders, swings, and tunnels. The building materials were piled up and we played on them. There were huge railroad ties scattered about—the large pieces of wood treated with creosote that support the steel rails of a railroad track. Our class decided to build something of our own until the construction workers needed them for their project. We would use the two-hundred-pound Lincoln Logs to build a cabin.

The stacking part was fun but dangerous—one of us could easily have lost a finger or some toes. Again, we did this *on* the playground with teachers watching us. I have no idea why we were allowed to do it, but we were.

After about a week, on the day we were to finish the project, there was excitement in the air. We rushed to our work site to slide the last of the ties onto what we called the roof, creating a secure box that could capably house a lion or a bear. The spaces between the ties were only about five or six inches apart, so once the last roof tie was set on, there would be no way out.

I was on the crew to carry the last huge piece of wood to be slid on the top. Josh Miller and I were lifting that final beam. He had come to our school that year and did not fit in, and I suspect he was happy to be included in the project. We were putting on the last piece and the gaggle of girls observing shouted out, "Chely, Josh, get inside of it, and that way you can lift from underneath." We hopped inside. The girls up on the roof slid it shut. We were trapped. They taunted me from above, then began spitting on us, leaving it on my face, my hands and arms, and in my hair.

The bell rang and everyone took off running to the classroom door. Not only was I angry about being trapped, the taunting, and the spit, but there was no way I was going to be late getting in that line. Without Josh's assistance, I moved a railroad tie enough to squeeze myself up and out of my cage. My classroom was in an annex just off of the main school building, so it didn't take long for me to run and get in the line. The girls gathered near the end of the line and laughed at me. I heard Jane say,

"Don't ignore me. I know you can hear me. Turn around when I'm talking to you. Chely is scared. You're scared!!" I was covered in spit and dirt and was not about to turn around and let them see me cry. Then Jane instructed one of the others to make me turn around.

I continued to focus on the door handle. Then someone shoved me hard from behind. With a movement similar to whiplash, I crashed forward into the door handle, hit my chin and lip, and slid down the wall. I didn't stay down long. I turned around, charged the entire group of girls without a single concern of who my victim would be. I beat one girl and left marks and blood on another.

My mother and Jane's mother were called to the school for a meeting with Mr. Peterson. Predictably, Jane's entire demeanor changed and she became submissive and polite to the adults. "Oh, I'm not sure *what* happened," she said. "I didn't see everything. I just saw Chely hitting those girls. I think it was a misunderstanding, but I'm not sure." Jane's mother offered my mother her opinion: I was too sensitive, and my mother needed to teach her kids to have a thicker skin. She said, "Chely, what you need to do when someone points out one of your flaws is to pick out a flaw that they have and say that back to them. If they have a big nose, just say, 'Well, your nose is too big,' and they'll stop picking on you. Just point out what's wrong with them." She told me that her daughter and the other girls weren't picking on me—they were just doing what kids do. She turned to my mom and said, "Don't you think that's the thing for Chely to do?" "No, I absolutely do not think that I want my daughter to pick out someone's insecurity or weakness and throw it back in their face. No, that's not what we'll be doing." My mother turned to Mr. Peterson and said, "I've got a load of laundry in the washer and I've gotta get it hung on the line, so I'm going to go home now." Mr. Peterson excused us all.

I was bullied for no reason at all, but the torment caused so much pain and fear that I often considered not going to school at all. Perhaps I would have become withdrawn, or fallen behind in academics. Young gay students have an added strike against them when their schoolmates who are bullies identify another reason to single them out and push them to the margins of society.

Underwater

Growing up, there were times when I believed that bad things happened to those I loved because of my sexuality. It was God's punishment for my being gay. It was my fault that the Old House burned down, that my parents couldn't stop fighting, that Uncle Earl was killed in a trucking accident. When my brother, Chris, broke his arm and shoulder and cracked his head open in a bike wreck, it was my fault. When my sister, Jeny, crashed her bike and needed dozens of stitches in her leg and face, it was my fault. These were messages of disapproval from the Lord Himself. That was the fire-and-brimstone God who berated me in church. Yet at the same time I knew that there was another, kinder God—one who knew and loved me and was on my side.

After the Old House had been reduced to ashes, we moved to a double-wide trailer on a three-acre plot surrounded by horse pasture outside of Wellsville. By then, I was talking regularly to both Gods in prayer. In church we'd pray for people who put their names on the prayer list—for so-and-so's grandma's bad hip or someone's husband who'd had a heart attack. And I'd created the special prayer that I knew that I couldn't ask to be put on any prayer list: *Please, God, don't let me be gay.* I began saying it every day, three times a day. I did the math: Saying the prayer approximately 1,095 times per year. Multiply that by three years and that's 3,285. That should've worked, I thought. That's many more times than we'd ever prayed for a hip or a liver. Then it occurred to me what I had been doing wrong. I had been saying my prayer silently, in my head. I knew that I needed to speak it, to say it out loud, like we did in church.

Several times a day, after school and into the evening, I'd head out to my "spot," a huge pasture behind our trailer where eight horses roamed. I'd walk out into the middle of that pasture, where I knew that no one could possibly hear me, and speak my prayer. I'd often get back to the house and feel the need to turn around and do it all over again. Sometimes I got yelled at by Mom for taking off when there were chores to do. But my new approach to the prayer was far more important, and it filled me with hope. No one knew about my secret except those eight horses.

But it wasn't enough to change me, or to spare those close to me. One Saturday morning, when I was ten, I heard my mother talking in hushed tones on the telephone to Aunt Char. She hung up, went to the back bedroom, and got my dad. Within a few minutes they'd piled us all into our Plymouth station wagon and headed to Aunt Char's place in Kansas City. Our cousin David had unexpectedly been admitted to the hospital. He was thirteen, the second oldest in our mob of five cousins, and he and his sister, Carey, then nine, were as close to me as siblings. We played together, got spankings together. We were given nearly identical new pairs of pajamas to wear on Christmas Eve. We shared bathwater, underwear, beds, and parents.

While the adults played pinochle or poker in the kitchen, we cousins got into trouble. Carey was famous for swiping a pair of scissors and cutting her own bangs, with predictable results (to this day, I still scan Carey's hairline to see if she's been hacking away at her locks again). Jeny and David were the ringleaders who would corral the younger kids into capers like climbing onto the roof of Aunt Char's house or lighting something on fire.

The only straight arrow among us was my brother, Chris, who would never tell a lie. David was wild enough to put Jeny into a clothes dryer, turn it on, and walk away. Despite any mischief, David was a shining star in our family. Aunt Char was a busy single mom and not a regular churchgoer, so David would take himself to services and Sunday school. He was a gifted violinist, and we often played music together. He was also a diabetic. David kept to a special diet, had to have snacks, peed on little sticks, and gave himself shots. Initially, the idea of his being in the hospital didn't throw us. I remember my mother telling us as we sped along the interstate early that summer morning, "He'll be all right. They just have to get his insulin levels straightened out and then he'll be fine. Don't worry."

At the hospital, Dad took us to the waiting room and bought us one bottle of Pepsi to share. Hours went by. Then Dad went

Christmas Day 1974

My parents and my aunt Char never missed a chance to line us all up, oldest to youngest, when they took our picture. Chris (age 6), Jeny (age 5), David (age 5), me (age 4), and Carey (age 2).

upstairs for what seemed like forever. When he returned, we asked after David. "He's very sick and if he doesn't start to get better within the next couple of hours, he could get worse," my father said. "I'm going to take you kids to Aunt Char's so the babysitter can leave." Carey had been at home with a neighbor the whole day, and Dad told us on the drive there not to tell her how ill her brother was. After he dropped us off, he headed back to the hospital. We asked our little cousin what she wanted to do, and she suggested we all go swimming. There was a public pool within walking distance, but we needed money to get in. So Carey went into David's room, took the little rubber stopper off the bottom of his piggy bank, and took out a few dollars.

All day I'd been dying to say my prayer. I had wanted to on the drive to Kansas City, at the hospital, and in Aunt Char's bathroom. But I was afraid to risk it. So once I got to the pool, I jumped in and stayed underwater most of the time. I prayed underwater that day. I didn't just speak the prayer. I screamed it. I was just so afraid that God had made David sick because of me. I came up for air, but then I'd just go back under and stay under. Over and over, I'd come up for a breath, then dive back down and pray. We didn't stay at the pool long. After we got home and changed out of our damp suits, the big station wagon pulled into the driveway with Mom, Aunt Char, and Dad in it.

We all ran to the front door full of questions. "Where's David?" My mom stared at the four of us blankly and said, "He died," as if she were talking about the weather. That night we went to Godfather's Pizza for supper. Aunt Char, Carey, and the rest of us sat at two tables with red-checkered tablecloths eating pizza and drinking pitchers of flat, warm Pepsi.

My prayer had failed me again.

Let Me Sing for You

On the back porch of our house out in the country in Wellsville, Kansas. 1983.
Left to right: Carey, Jeny, me, Chris.

I started getting paid to sing and play piano when I was eleven, not long after David died. If there was no money to be paid, but there was a willing audience, I performed anyway. I'd haul my keyboard, an amp, and a microphone to bars, VFW halls, auto shop openings, picnics, weddings, funerals, hospitals, schools, churches, and living rooms. But my specialty was nursing homes.

I had landed my first official gig years before, when we were still living in the Old House. The way my parents tell it, I was four years old, roaming free in our yard, when all of a sudden I disappeared. My folks searched the shed, the chicken coop, and under the big gray porch. Then they started to panic. Neighbors canvassed the neighborhood and finally found me six blocks away at the Wellsville Manor nursing home, playing their piano and singing songs to a couple of residents in wheelchairs.

After my parents got me home that night, they asked me where I had learned to play the piano. They say that I informed them that I always knew I could; I just needed a piano in the house and I'd play for them too. In my short life leading up to that day, I had spent many hours sitting on the lap of my great-grandmother, Melvina Dixon, as she played old-time church music on her upright piano. I can still see her and the light blue veins that crawled in her translucent, pale hands. I'd put my tiny hands right on top of hers as she played. I told her once, "Grandma, I can do that." To which she replied, "I know you can."

Later, my folks inherited Grandma Dixon's piano and it became my best friend. My folks asked me if I wanted to take formal piano lessons and I said yes. They didn't have extra money for such an expense, but they scraped some together and saw to it that I had a chance to properly learn my instrument.

My first piano teacher told me that I had perfect hands for playing piano. I have long, skinny fingers that I've always been a little self-conscious about. Running them up and down the keyboard has always been as natural as breathing.

As a kid, I'd listen for new songs on 61 Country AM, remember the tunes, and run to the piano and play them. My dad's coon-hunting buddies were always around the house, and I'd tug at their Carhart coveralls and make them sit by me while I played. Once I even convinced a Kirby vacuum cleaner salesman who showed up at our door to attend a private concert (my mom bought the vacuum cleaner, too).

One day when I was five, Rev. Skiles, the Baptist preacher, came to call, and I asked him if he wanted to hear the latest song I'd mastered. He obliged. I sat down on the piano bench and patted the empty spot next to me. I played the song perfectly and when I finished, I turned to him and asked, "Whaddya think, Warren?" All he could say was "Wow." At that moment my mom walked into the room and asked what I'd been serenading the minister with.

" 'Love in the Hot Afternoon'!" I declared with pride. I watched the color drain out of my mother's face as she realized that her young daughter had just sung the 1975 Gene Watson hit about a tawdry, midday sexual encounter between two strangers to our preacher.

. . . .

That we fell right to sleep
In the damp tangled sheets so soon
After love in the hot afternoon

As I got older, the performances got better and my audiences got bigger. By the time I was eleven, I began to get calls to come play with bands or to play solo. I also found my way to Opry shows—regional country music concerts modeled after the Grand Ole Opry and often broadcast live on the radio. These shows drew large audiences of country fans who would drive for miles to hear their favorite music. Typically, I'd perform three or four songs with a house band of seasoned musicians. Kansas City had a popular show called the Farris Opry, owned and operated by a musician named Byron Jones. I had a burning passion to land a guest spot on his show.

If you successfully auditioned for a slot on one Opry show,

others were likely to book you as well. In that way you could build a regional following, and I knew that if I ever wanted to make it in Nashville, I'd have to be able to make it big in Kansas City first. It seemed to me that the Farris Opry, just an hour up the pike in Kansas City, held the keys to my success. By my early teens, I had enough of a name playing around Kansas and Missouri for Byron to allow me to come up for a special closed audition.

My parents never pushed me into entertainment, but when I asked them to drive me wherever I needed to go, they did. So they happily took me up to Kansas City. The plan was for me to do my audition, join my folks for dinner at a restaurant, then come back to the theater to enjoy the Opry that night. I hoped that if things went well, I'd be back in a month or two as a featured guest, so catching the show that night would be homework for the future.

I performed a few songs, backed up by the house band, which was led by Byron's son Kevin. He was the best guitar player that I'd ever heard live in my life. After I sang, Byron asked me a lot of questions as he stood in the center aisle of the auditorium. When we wrapped up, he chatted with my parents by the concession stand and asked if we were going to grab a quick bite to eat. We said yes and asked him for a restaurant recommendation. He gave one, but added, "Be sure to get back here by the start of the show, 'cause you're going on in the second slot." I about jumped out of my skin. I was going to be singing live on Kansas City radio while performing on the stage of the Farris Opry that very night, in front of a sold-out crowd! My parents were happy for me and we went off to that restaurant. I don't think I ate a bite.

Salisbury Steak, Please

It was around this time that I received one of many signs from God. When I was about twelve years old, I started to explore the notion that I had a birth defect—a big one.

I began to consider the possibility that I was actually supposed to have been born a boy. I was good at sports, I liked to play outdoors, and I thought that girls were pretty. So, naturally, I'd been praying really hard to God, asking Him to give me a sign to let me know how to go about addressing what I now believed to be a birth defect.

I went with my family to the only sit-down restaurant in Wellsville for dinner one evening. This was a rare occurrence for us—to actually get to go out to eat. I was excited and I knew just what I wanted to order: the Salisbury Steak Dinner. We were seated and our waitress came to our table with a tray of ice water. We knew her. Everyone knew everyone in that town, but we knew her as a friend of the family.

She had played on the high school girls' softball team that my mom and dad had coached a year or so before. She started making small talk with my folks, talking about school and her new softball team. I was seated nearer to her than my folks were; they were next to the wall in the booth and I was the closest to where she stood. Her leg kept bumping my leg as she chatted and laughed next to me.

She held the empty ice-water tray over my head as if it was a little shelter she'd built for me. Because I was seated and she was standing, I was on eye level with her breasts. I looked at them, in her tight T-shirt, and then I forced myself to look away. It wasn't right, I thought to myself. There must be something wrong with me. I was born in the wrong body. I was defective. I told myself not to look again, but I couldn't resist. I checked to see if my brother was staring at her chest, too. He wasn't. He was busy trying to blow the paper wrapper off of the drinking straw into the light fixture dangling above our heads.

I suppose our waitress informed my family about the dinner specials that night, but I can't be sure. After being fixated on those breasts for a good two minutes—a long time for a twelve-year-old girl in Wellsville, Kansas, to be staring at a seventeen-year-old girl's boobs—I got a sign. I finally actually noticed the words ironed onto her T-shirt. Written in red capital letters was the message GOD DON'T MAKE MISTAKES.

I felt, on that night, that I was okay. I had hope and some comfort, for a while at least, that I was just as I was supposed to be.

The beautiful young waitress turned to me and asked me for my order, and I shouted, a little too enthusiastically, "Salisbury Steak Dinner, please!"

She smiled. "Okay, sweetie," replied God's buxom, cheerful messenger. Then she tapped me on the head with her pencil and bounced off toward the kitchen.

The Boy on a Tractor

By my teens, I was looking hard to find anyone who was like me. I knew a few girls who were considered stereotypically tough and tomboyish, but they had boyfriends. I didn't fit the stereotype of a gay woman, but I knew my sexual identity was outside the norm. I hadn't heard many discussions about homosexuality, but what I heard in church was enough for me to realize that the church did not approve.

There was one person in Wellsville who I thought was gay—a single man in his thirties named Sam. I never saw him with a boyfriend, but some people called him our town pervert. I assumed the only way he could have earned such contempt would have been to be a homosexual, though I never asked about it. I just knew I didn't want to join him.

Faced with the possibility of life as an outcast, I tried hard to develop feelings for boys, with no luck. That is, until Loren Gretencord moved to town. I wonder if I was drawn to Loren because of his unisex name or the fact that he was so pretty. Not merely handsome, but beautiful—with smooth skin, full lips, long eyelashes, and wavy blond hair. In fact, I thought he was prettier than any girl in Wellsville Junior High. He was two years ahead of me, but we were cast together in the school play. I wrote Loren a love letter, and I asked my sister to give it to him, enclosing a school picture and asking him to go out with me.

Days went by without a response. Loren didn't look at me in the hallway and didn't act any differently toward me at rehearsal. It was mortifying. I just knew that the other kids in school had read my letter and were going to make fun of me. I recently asked my sister, "What ever happened to that letter I asked you to give to Loren Gretencord? Did you even give it to him?" She snickered and said, "Of course not, silly."

With my love life stalled, I focused on music, basketball, schoolwork, and chores. Had I been into boys, I would've made a lot more time for them. But when I was about to turn fifteen, I met Mike Folks. It was toward the end of summer, and I was driving down Main Street to pick something up for my mother (at that time, kids in Kansas could get their driver's license at the age of fourteen, but they were only allowed to get behind the wheel without an adult if they were running "farm errands"). I was in my mom and dad's old beat-up truck when I noticed that there was a big tractor in front of me at the flashing red light.

When the young man driving the tractor turned at the signal, the wind picked up and blew the ball cap off his head and it landed in the street. He'd made an attempt to grab it as it went airborne, but he was in mid-turn on a big piece of farm equipment. Even though there were a few cars behind me, I switched off my ignition, got out of the truck, and picked up the cap. But the young man on the tractor didn't see me retrieve it, and he kept on driving.

I followed in the truck. He finally stopped, and I pulled up behind him. I ran up to him just as he was climbing off the tractor. I said, "Hey, you dropped your hat." He flashed a big smile, and I explained how I'd retrieved it. I was well aware that Mike had been a star player on our high school football team. Now he was studying at nearby Ottawa University and was playing football there.

"I've seen you play basketball a couple of times," he said to me. "You're pretty good." I was flattered and then told him I needed to get home. When I got back to the truck, I noticed he hadn't moved from the spot beside his tractor. He didn't smile or wave. He just stood there, with the rescued cap in his hand, looking back at me.

A few days later, I saw Mike again. I had been working on Sundays at East Kansas Chemical, a convenience store that also sold wholesale farm supplies and served as a gas station. I could work only on Sundays because I was underage and the store didn't sell beer on Sunday. The owners, Bonnie and Carl Coffman, would open the store early on Sunday morning and I would take over at 11:00 a.m. I stocked shelves, mopped, inventoried, and logged the sales of fuel by the hundreds of gallons. I loved Carl and Bonnie, who let me prove myself at a grown-up job.

Mike walked into the store and waited until I was through serving customers. "I found you," he said, once the store had grown quiet and it was just the two of us standing there. I was embarrassed and didn't know what to say—surely he hadn't come in there just to see me? Indeed, he had. It was the beginning of a cherished relationship that lasted through much of my teens.

I began dating Mike. I wanted to measure up to other girls my age, and they were starting to have physical relationships with boys. My friends would complain about how hard it was to resist going all the way with a boy, how things would just be getting going and they'd get caught up in how good it felt. It was as if they were speaking another language.

Mike and I had a pretty traditional courtship. When he wasn't in class or at football practice in Ottawa, he'd come to Wellsville to see me. His parents were great to be around, and we'd eat family dinners with them whenever we could. I liked how important family was to him, and I especially loved how he doted on his nephew Phillip. After family dinners, Mike would drive me over to his college and we'd spend time at the house he shared with his friends. He showed great respect for me, but like any guy his age he wanted to move things along sexually, and I dreaded that. I actually liked kissing, but making out with Mike managed to both bore and frighten me. Attempts to do more than kissing always ended awkwardly. I'm sure Mike thought that I was being a good girl and showing restraint, and he never ever made me feel bad for not giving in, even though he was by no means a virgin. Still, he once hurt me terribly by cheating on me with a girl named Michelle, who was known around town. I've always thought he did it out of frustration, and in a way Michelle took the pressure off of me.

Mike and I dated on and off while I was in high school. At some point during my junior year, I began dating Andrew Collins. Andrew was the starting quarterback of his football team in Gardner, just a couple of exits up I-35. I'm not sure what Andrew saw in me, since he could have had any girl in that rural part of Kansas. I even wondered if he dated me because he'd taken a bet from his buddies to see if he could go all the way with me. If so, he lost.

Like Mike, Andrew wound up cheating on me, in this case with one of my oldest childhood friends, Erin McAlpin. I suspected something was going on between them, but both denied it. Then one day I was at Andrew's house, waiting for him in his room while he took a quick shower. I wasn't snooping, but I saw a handful of letters folded into neat squares on his dresser. On the outside of each square, "Andrew" was written in feminine handwriting. I opened one, glanced at the bottom to see who had signed it, saw her name, and then read the letter. I read every one, managing to carry on a conversation with Andrew as he dressed in the bathroom. After, I walked out of his house, got in my car, and drove home before he'd even come out and faced me. Andrew called, but I never spoke to him again.

Sometime the next week, at school, Erin asked me if we could go outside and talk about it. She admitted what had happened, but insisted on showing me letters Andrew had written to her, too. She wanted me to know that they were both guilty. She asked for my forgiveness and I gave it without hesitation. I was upset, but not for the reason one might imagine. I wasn't hurt that my boyfriend and one of my best friends had betrayed me. I was upset because I didn't really care what he did or who he did it with. No matter how hard I tried, I couldn't feel anything like heartbreak over losing a boy. I was upset that I wasn't upset enough.

The Ozark Jubilee

Between my junior and senior years of high school, I moved away from home to chase my dreams of country music fame at the Ozark Jubilee. The Jubilee was one of the hottest live shows in Branson, Missouri, and I'd successfully auditioned to be a featured singer. It had a great history of presenting artists like Porter Wagoner, Red Foley, and Brenda Lee. Back in 1988, Branson was still a quaint little resort, the perfect place for me to try living the life of a performer.

I got the gig after playing around the area and making a name for myself. Tony James, a Branson music promoter, saw me and suggested that I participate in his talent shows. I won a couple of them and I lost a couple of them, but Tony believed in me and recommended me to Clifford and Maggie Sue Campbell, the owners of the Jubilee. They trusted his instinct and agreed to give me an audition.

Branson was five hours from Wellsville. I was seventeen and hadn't saved up enough money for my own car, so my parents took me up to Branson for my audition. We arrived at the theater a couple of hours early to be safe. No one was there yet, so I hopped out of the car and got my picture taken standing in front of the building. I still have that snapshot. At my audition, it became clear that the other Jubilee performers—all of them seasoned musicians in their thirties—weren't thrilled about playing with a teenager. The band grudgingly went through the motions onstage with me. At one point, Clifford asked me to go over to the piano and play with the band while someone else sang. I was able to follow along with relative ease and sing the harmony parts.

Mom, Dad, and I returned to Wellsville, and not long after that the Campbells called and offered me a job. I was excited but overwhelmed. I would need to find a place to live, buy a car, and move to Branson.

I ended up renting a mobile home sight unseen in a trailer park called Yeller Holler, about fifteen minutes from Branson's strip, where the Jubilee and other big theaters were. I bought my first car, a 1976 Plymouth Duster, for $600. I threw my keyboard, my boom box, and all of my clothes in that hideous car and headed down to the Ozarks. Mom rode with me to help me settle in, and Dad came up a few days later to drive her back to Wellsville. I didn't have a lot of stuff. The trailer had a bed and a kitchen table with no chairs. I was moved in no time flat.

The next day I had a show at the Jubilee. The only thing I had to wear onstage was my hot-pink lamé prom dress that I had debuted in Wellsville a couple weeks before. It had cost $180, and I was thrilled to get to put it to use more than once. After a couple of shows, the veteran members of the cast warmed up to me. In the end, they all proved to be kind and generous, and they taught me so much about performing and how to treat fans.

That summer was unbelievably hot, and my trailer had no air-conditioning. The little thermometer duct-taped to the paneling in the living room would sometimes hit more than 120 degrees. I wasn't required to be at the theater each day until about four o'clock, but I'd often get there two hours early just to take advantage of the cool sixty-four-degree air that blasted through the Jubilee. With my parents back in Wellsville, Clifford and Maggie looked after me, but I reveled in being on my own. There wasn't a telephone in my trailer, so every Wednesday I'd call home from a gas station pay phone at the bottom of the hill from Yeller Holler. The one time I forgot, my parents drove all night to check on me.

During my time in Branson, I again found myself attracted to another girl. I'd hoped that somehow moving to a new town in a new state would end what was tormenting me. Because I lived alone in my trailer, I could say my prayer again and again and no one would overhear it. And one night I thought God must've heard me.

During our two-hour show there was an intermission, and the performers would usually stand at the front of the stage and sign autographs. The audience was usually an older crowd, so if young folks did show up, the entire cast noticed. One night, three handsome, athletic-looking boys my age waited after the first half of the show to talk to me. They said they were on a road trip before their first year in college and that this was the best

My best friends in high school. Left to right: Christy, Deb, me, Susan, and Tina.

part of their adventure so far. They hailed from Olive Branch, Mississippi, a little town near Memphis. They reminded me of the boys from my hometown—particularly the boy called Augie. We made our small talk, and then I had to get back to work. During the show I found my eyes wandering to the section where Augie and his pals were seated. I was so excited to have people my age in the audience.

Afterward, I was backstage putting my dresses and shoes away when Clifford came to tell me that Augie and Co. were still out there and wanted to see me again. "They asked me if it was all right if they invited you to go get some ice cream," he said. "I told them that if you do go with them, there had better be no funny business or they'll have to answer to me." I thanked Clifford and accepted the invitation.

Being in Branson was like living on the grounds of a giant amusement park, so we all went to ride go-carts. During the evening, Augie revealed that they couldn't afford a hotel, so they'd pitched a tent at a local campground. He asked if we could go back to my trailer. I agreed, even though I knew my parents would have killed me; my gut told me that they were good guys. Since I had only one chair, we all sat on the floor and listened to cassette tapes of my favorite country music. I had no snacks or soda to offer, but they didn't mind, and we talked until about three in the morning. Then I said I had to get some sleep. The boys hopped to their feet and thanked me for visiting with them. I asked them where their campsite was and if they had enough blankets and sleeping bags. Augie explained that they had only two sleeping bags for the three of them. I couldn't let one of them shiver in the cold all night in some tent, so I invited the entire crew to spend the night in my trailer's second bedroom, where there was a queen-size bed and enough blankets for one boy to sleep comfortably on the floor. They behaved like gentlemen and left early the next morning.

About ten days later I got a thank-you letter in the mail from

*My senior picture, Class of '89. I didn't
want to spend my money on having my
senior picture taken because I was saving
for my move to Nashville, but I'm
glad I went ahead and did it.*

Augie and was struck by how thoughtful he was. We became pen pals, and during his first spring break from Ole Miss, later that year, he borrowed his sister's car without asking and drove to see me in Kansas. Soon we were dating. We continued to see each other even after I graduated from high school and moved to Nashville. Initially I was hopeful that Augie's appearance at the Jubilee was divine intervention, designed to save me from homosexuality. But soon I was wrestling with my old fears again. Nothing could save me from being gay.

Opryland USA, 1989

In May of 1989 I began my new job as a singer at Opryland USA. The theme park no longer exists, but at one time it was a thriving and beloved part of Nashville's tourism. I was hired to be one of sixteen performers in an outdoor show called *Country Music USA,* a fast-paced musical revue of country music's past and present. I've never had more fun in my life.

Because it was so fast-paced, the performers had to make multiple costume changes backstage in a matter of seconds. People were hired specifically to help us get in and out of costumes. The changing area backstage was cramped, but all of us became close friends, including the dressers, the band, and the crew. There were nine boys and seven girls in the show, and each of us had worked hard to get there. Thousands of young people from all over the nation had auditioned for a spot on that show, and we were the fortunate sixteen who got hired.

For years I'd been a big fish in a small pond, and now that was changing. Not only was I hired to sing solos but I needed to learn how to sing in a chorale environment. When I did well, it bolstered my confidence to know that there were very few things that I couldn't learn how to be somewhat good at. One of the things I realized was that I could never be great at dancing.

I did the dance rehearsals every day and I knew them step for step. They were complicated and confusing, but I was deter-

This statue of Roy Acuff and Minnie Pearl sits in the lobby of the Ryman Auditorium in Nashville, Tennessee, the original home of the Grand Ole Opry. I played the role of Minnie Pearl in the Country Music USA *show. Several years later, the artist commissioned to sculpt the statue had me "sit and pose" for reference photos because I knew Minnie's mannerisms and had the "Minnie dress and hat." Shortly before Miss Minnie passed away, I visited her and she thanked me. Her husband, Henry, had taken pictures of the statue to show her and she was pleased with the result.*

mined to do my job. There were group dances that I was required to perform for every show. There were also other dance numbers that were assigned to the more qualified and skilled dancers. Even if a person in the show wasn't cast in the more difficult dances, we still had to know them in case someone became sick or injured. For the majority of my years at Opryland, I was spared the humiliation of my lack of dancing ability, but I gained a tremendous respect for other people's gift of performance, and that has served me well over the years.

One of the guys in the show was particularly extraordinary, as a dancer and as a vocalist. His name was Ray Kinman, and he was a star of our show on and off the stage. We were all relatively outgoing and enjoyed kidding around, but Ray was a ham. He was intelligent, quick-witted, and willing to do just about anything for a laugh. We made up skits, did monologues and dialogues, created characters, and made everything in our tiny world seem funny.

Ray was a young gay man from Alabama who used sarcasm and comedy to deflect any blow that came his way.

I was a little bit timid around Ray because he was so clever and smart. He and I had never really had a confrontation, mostly because I was the new kid in the show and there was an unspoken hierarchy at Opryland.

Then one day, in between shows, he and I happened to be in the backstage area re-setting our costumes for the next performance. Each cast member had about six assigned hooks on the wall, and with the help of our dressers we'd make our lightning-quick costume changes next to our hooks.

Ray and I were making small talk and tidying up our respective areas when one of the other guys in the show came up behind him and playfully slapped him on the backside. Ray quipped to the other guy as he trotted off, "I know you want me, you big queen." I must've made a noise or given a look of disapproval because Ray asked me, "What's your problem?" I told him that I didn't appreciate having to witness things like that. We got into a discussion about homosexuality. I told him that I thought it was a sin, a deviant behavior that someone chooses, and that the Bible supported my position. I told him that I didn't care what he did or who he was, but I asked him to please not do it around me. His face turned red in anger and frustration as he tried to explain to me that it was not a choice for him. He went on to tell me that I was ignorant and I was not in Kansas anymore. As he walked off, he said, "You better get used to it. Opryland is full of fags."

I felt bad for saying what I'd said to him, and I felt bad for myself too. My experience in Branson the summer before had scared me in a whole new way. I wanted another brand-new start. I was disappointed that I had not been able to leave my homosexuality behind the summer before, and I'd made up my mind to dedicate myself to changing. Not only did I truly want to change—I didn't want to be discovered by other gays. I'd never been around anyone whom I knew to be gay. I had an overwhelming fear that they might see "it" in me. I didn't know any better. I thought that I could, without realizing it, have some characteristic or trait that other gays might be able to identify.

Years later, I heard from a friend of a friend that Ray had told people that I was gay. He did have reason to say that, by the way. He'd been aware of a friendship that I had with a girl whom they all suspected of being gay, and she was. I suppose that my hateful rant against homosexuality in those first few weeks at Opryland only fueled his speculation about me. As I have grown older, I have paid attention to those who are so overtly opposed to and vocal against homosexuality, especially those who prop up their arguments with the Bible. An educated guess tells me that some of them who rant are actually gay.

Ray and I enjoyed a good friendship for years, even though I kept him at arm's length. There were times when I wanted to confide in him, and there were times over the years when I desperately needed him. I'm hopeful that I can find Ray Kinman and ask his forgiveness.

Brenda

Ｏne of the only things I knew for certain when I moved to Nashville was that I had three months of employment. My contract with Opryland was for the summer of 1989, but that short contract was my ticket to Nashville.

The Opryland casts were seasonal workers, but some casts had longer contracts than others. The Opryland management assigned a color to the different groups. I was in the Blue Cast, and our contract was only for the summer months. The more-seasoned cast was called the Red Cast. In theory, the Opryland higher-ups would choose performers at the end of the summer from Red and Blue to constitute the group of performers who would get to have employment into the fall months. They called this the Purple Cast. It was understood, however, that if anyone in Red chose to stay and be in Purple, they had seniority.

Most of us in Blue wanted to continue on with the show, but we had heard through the grapevine that we didn't have a shot. It seemed that only one performer from the Red Cast was choosing to leave the show. Randy Harrell had been one of the veteran performers at the park for years, and he had decided that it was time for him to pursue other career opportunities, so only one male performer from Blue would get to be in Purple. We Blue Cast members were happy that our friend Ken Mellons would get to be the one to fill that spot. That said, the rest of us were all worried about how we'd be able to pay our bills in the coming months. A few kids from our group were headed back to their home states to attend college, but most of us had rolled the dice on our dreams to get to Nashville and would have done most anything to keep from having to pack up and leave. I knew that if I found myself out of work I had no options back home, and I was not going to move back to Kansas. Some of my cast mates knew that if they got really down and out they could borrow money from their parents. I didn't have that luxury.

We were each in charge of retrieving our many different costumes from the wardrobe trailer, which sat directly behind the theater. Every day I'd load up my six or seven different costumes, including shoes and boots. As I walked up the back stairs of the theater, one of the crew guys was walking down the steps, eating a popular Opryland treat called Dippin' Dots, a cup filled with tiny multicolored ice cream balls the size of BB's. "Congratulations," he said, as he spat two of the Dippin' Dots on my face. "Oops, sorry," he said, as we passed one another on the stairs and kept walking. My stage manager asked me if I'd known prior to the announcement. I didn't know what he was talking about. That was a remarkable day for me. A few minutes before I arrived at the theater, the Purple Cast list had been posted and I was the only Blue Cast member other than Ken who was promoted to the Purple Cast. The worst had been confirmed for the rest of my cast members who were not on the list; their jobs at Opryland would be ending in a week. I quietly went about my day and accepted the heartfelt pats on the back from my peers.

There was little acceptance of me in the Purple Cast during the first two weeks. Ken was welcomed with great excitement and warmth because he was taking a spot from someone who chose to leave, but my situation was different. Every female in the Red Cast had wanted to stay on through the Purple season. The directors and creative staff of the show had made a decision not to renew one of the girls' contracts, and I was hired to move up. I hated how it felt to be unwelcome. All of the gals in Purple were older than me—I was eighteen and they were between twenty-two and thirty. A couple of the girls were overtly vocal about how much they didn't want me there and how unfair it was that their friend's contract didn't get renewed. I toughed it out and held my ground. Within two weeks of my joining the Purple Cast, things couldn't have been more different. I suppose they got tired of working so hard at excluding me, so they began to let me in. In no time, real friendships were forged, and some of those friendships have gone on.

I was lucky to have employment for those additional three months, but the park was scheduled to close for the season and I needed a job, any job, to get me through the winter.

I loved my job at Opryland USA as a performer in the Country Music USA *show. I wasn't a strong dancer, but I had fun and did the best I could. That's me smack-dab in the middle. 1991.*

I had moved from my furnished single-wide trailer into a house that was closer to downtown Nashville and closer to Opryland. Laura-Grace, her brother, Gardnar, and I ended up living together for years, and their entire family was as much a family to me as I'd ever known.

Laura-Grace and I were nineteen years old, and Gardnar was just a year younger than us. Their mom and dad lived in Kentucky but had purchased the house as an investment since they knew that their kids wanted to work and go to school in Nashville. I was told that I could have the basement bedroom, and I was thrilled with it. I asked Barbara, Laura-Grace's mom, if I could have permission to paint it. She encouraged me to treat the house as if it were my own. The room had dark wood paneling, so I bought two gallons of light blue paint and spent days rolling four coats of it on the walls; the paneling just soaked it up. Eventually it looked just how I wanted it to look. The three of us took great pride in that house; we'd have days where we power-cleaned it top to bottom. It was just so nice to have a beautiful, clean place to call home.

My bills were minimal, but I knew I needed to find a job immediately. I'd heard from the other young performers at Opryland that if all else failed, one could always get a job bagging groceries at Kroger, a well-known chain of grocers in the South.

After a four-show day at Opryland, I drove over to the strip mall near home and parked my car in front of the Kroger store that anchored the entire shopping center nearest my home. It was about nine in the evening when I asked the gal behind the service counter if I could fill out an application for employment. She picked up the store phone and summoned the manager. He appeared a few minutes later and told me that they weren't hiring. I asked if I could fill out an application in case a position should open up. The only position open at that time was the position of a butcher. I asked him if I should come back in a few days to see if applications were being taken then. He said it would be a waste of my time. I swallowed hard and thanked him.

The Kroger job was supposed to be a sure thing. I got into my yellow 1980 AMC Concord (the Banana) and sat for a minute. I put the key in the ignition and thought about my options. I had none. I had to find a job. I saw a store at the end of that strip mall that appeared to be open. I parked my car in the spot nearest the front door of the store called Sport Seasons. I saw that the sign on the door had been flipped around to display the SORRY, WE'RE CLOSED side of it. The man who was inside cleaning was squatting down behind the cash register counter. As soon as he stood upright, I knocked on the glass door. He jumped, and as he walked to the door he put his hand on his chest, signifying to me that I'd nearly given him a heart attack.

He got to the door and pointed at the sign and mouthed the words "We're closed." I said loudly that I realized they were closed but I just needed to ask him a question. He turned the key and said to come in, and he locked the door behind me. I stuck out my hand and introduced myself, asking him for his name. His name was Doug. I asked if I could fill out an application for employment. He started shaking his head from side to side before I was even able to finish my question. They weren't hiring, and if and when he made a new hire it would be someone with extensive retail experience in sporting goods. When he asked me if I had any qualifications like that, I was truthful, but I told him I could learn anything. I asked him if I could come back and talk to the manager during business hours, and he said, "I am the manager. Hell, I'm the owner, too."

Zero for two. I got in my car. I reached into my purse, grabbed one item, and walked right back up to that door. I knocked again. He was bent over a big cardboard box, and without standing, he looked in my direction and waved his hand at me to go away. I knocked again, this time harder, and he stood up. I held the item from my purse flat up against the window, and he squinted his eyes to see what it was that I was trying to show him. He shook his head in frustration but walked over to the door and unlocked it. He asked me, "What are you doing? What are you holding up to my window?" I showed it to him again. It was my checkbook. I showed him the balance register of my checkbook and asked if he'd give me one minute to tell him something. He asked if he had a choice.

I said if he would look closely at the balance of my checkbook he'd see that I had $13.33 left in my account. Then I committed the cardinal sin of being a wannabe entertainer trying to find employment to pay the bills. I told him that I had come to Nashville to be a famous country singer, that my job at Opryland was ending soon, and that I was dead set against moving back to Kansas. Then I suggested that I come and work for him for one week, starting the next day, for free. I declared that I was good at math, I had the ability to count people's change back to them, I had an excellent memory, I was good with people, and I was a hard worker. I said that I was finished with what I had to say. He finally threw his head back and groaned, "Okaaay." He told me to come back ready to work at ten o'clock the next morning.

The other employees were all helpful, professional, and welcoming. I had a crash course in stock codes, products, orders, returns, running credit cards, stacking, sorting, and pricing. Shortly before that first long day ended, I had to go to the back office to ask Doug a question about something. After he answered, I turned to walk back out to the front of the store. He said, "Come back tomorrow. You're hired." I spun around and said, "Thank you. I appreciate it more than you'll ever know." I worked for Sport Seasons for a couple of years, and that job got me through the leanest times.

When I knew for certain that I had the job, I felt a sense of triumph and a glimmer of hope. The way I saw it was this: if I had been able to find a job even when there wasn't one to be had, I was going to be able to parlay that luck into landing a record contract. Getting that job was a foreshadowing of my destiny—I was convinced of that.

There were six or seven employees at that time, but for the most part, three of us ran that store every day. Skid was a late-forty-something single father of one and was the most dependable and disciplined person I'd ever known.

Joy was the in-house bookkeeper, and when I started at the store, she was about eight months pregnant. She was helpful to me, but she stayed in the back most of the time, filling in numbers on the blank spaces of spreadsheets and signing checks.

Brenda was nineteen, just seven months older than me. She was a native Nashvillian and had worked for Doug long enough to have the freedom to stroll into work three minutes late every day. She was tall, tan, thin, and athletic, and she was blessed with long, pretty legs and a perfect white smile.

Brenda and I started to spend time together away from Sport Seasons. I liked to hear her speak and, more importantly, I liked to watch her speak. She had the prettiest teeth, and I was taken with the way her lips looked when she spoke in her slight Southern accent. She had a kind disposition, and everyone liked her. The boys flirted with her and tried to date her. She didn't flirt back with them much, I noticed. It seemed to me that she simply tolerated their advances and did her best not to lead them on.

We were spending all day together at the store, but I never grew tired of her company. After three or four weeks or so of knowing her, I wondered if she could sense that I had a crush. I did nothing and said nothing about it, of course. I'd developed crushes on girls before and knew that I just had to deal with the feelings privately and hope that they would fade away. I had no intention of making my feelings known. I had promised myself years before that I would never act on my homosexual inclinations. I wanted to have a successful career in music and I wanted to have a happy life. I was still working at Opryland, and I'd often been vocal with men in my cast about the sins of being gay. I was truly tortured and I knew that I was a hypocrite.

Brenda invited me to go to a party one Saturday night, and since it was the last weekend of Opryland for me, I told her that I didn't want to go out. I wanted to be fully rested for my Sunday performances. I'd been working with the cast and crew for months and we had all become close. It would be an emotional day and I wanted to be in top form.

I got home that Saturday night at 9:30 p.m. Brenda's car was in my driveway. She said she wanted to make sure I hadn't changed my mind. She suggested that I go for an hour or so and said she'd bring me right home after that. I was planning to take a shower and watch some TV in the basement. There was a makeshift living room downstairs by my bedroom, and although I was certainly allowed to watch TV upstairs in the main living room, I seldom did. I told Brenda that she was more than welcome to come in for a while before she went to the party.

I got out of my makeup, took a quick shower, put on sweatpants, and flopped on the couch. She had already been surfing the channels and found a movie that was just starting. We were sitting on the couch with our feet up on the coffee table. I turned the lamp off because it was causing a glare on the TV. Also, looking at Brenda made me nervous. I wondered why she was there. I knew that she was expected at that party. I wondered if she had a crush on me and if she was feeling scared about it. I was scared that she did have a crush on me. On the other hand, I was scared that she didn't.

I leaned away from her and put my head down on a pillow at the end of the couch. She invited me to put my legs in her lap, so I did. After a few minutes she asked if she could lie next to me. The couch was deep enough for two people, and I said yes.

She stretched out directly behind me and we covered up with

a blanket. Since the day we'd met, I'd loved how Brenda smelled, and I'd come to associate her perfume with a feeling of excitement. I breathed in her scent as if it were a cloud of gold dust, shimmering with little specks of magic that made me feel like I'd never felt before. It was the first time I'd ever had a girl's body pressed against mine, and I was sure that she could hear and feel the pounding in my chest. She slid her arm around my waist and pulled me even closer to her. I was thankful that we weren't facing each other and looking into each other's eyes.

I felt her breathing on the back of my neck. Her heartbeat thumped between my shoulder blades. I'd been with boys before in similar situations, and I'd heard their breathing get heavy with excitement. It had always been easy for me in situations with boys who begged me to go further or to go all the way with them. I just said no every time. I was able to say no not because I was a good girl brimming with virtue and restraint, ready to resist the urges of physical pleasure for reasons of morality but simply because I was not aroused. I was never tempted. My heart never pounded, my breathing never changed, the private parts of my body never made themselves known with an urging for me to keep going, keep going. But now everything was different.

I didn't have a fear that Laura-Grace or Gardnar would come downstairs and interrupt. It was nearly midnight. I'd already heard the familiar sounds of their bedroom doors being closed for the night, and there was a part of me that knew I needed to be drifting off to sleep as well. Every day at Opryland was a physical challenge. We performed four shows a day, and the added emotion of our last day would be draining. There I was—anything but sleepy.

I felt her lips gently touch my right ear. I rolled over onto my back, and with our faces now just inches from one another, I quietly said, "I'm scared." "It's okay, it's just a kiss," she whispered. Our lips touched, softly.

In my efforts to avoid going all the way with boys, kissing had become my specialty. Until that night with Brenda on the couch, kissing had been a menial chore that I performed.

My body was in full command, feeling things and doing things that I'd never known it to do. In the hours that followed, I started to understand conversations that I'd been a part of during high school. When other girls in my class and I would have "girl talk," they'd go on about how difficult it was for them to say no to their boyfriends. I had often judged them for not resisting the temptations of sexual activity. Suddenly, I had a new and enlightened understanding. In the early hours of that morning, I felt whole.

Brenda left my house around three o'clock in the morning. I fell asleep for a few hours. There was a beautiful antique mahogany wardrobe in my bedroom that belonged to Laura-Grace's mom. It had shelves and drawers and a place to hang clothes. There was also a long, vertical door with a full-length dressing mirror, and when I awakened every morning and opened my eyes, the first thing I would see was the reflection of my face in that mirror. The morning after Brenda, when I realized that I had, indeed, been with a girl, I stared at myself in that beveled antique mirror. I wondered if this was a first for that hundred-year-old mirror. Was this the first time that a young girl of nineteen had ever stared helplessly into it the morning after having been consumed by passion for another girl?

I cried until it was time to get up. I showered, made my lunch, and drove myself to work. I usually listened to the radio during the thirty-minute commute to the park. My car had only an AM radio, and that was just fine with me because the station that I listened to—650 WSM-AM—was the home of the Grand Ole Opry. I didn't even think to turn it on that morning. Instead I replayed a lot of what had happened the night before. Blood rushed to my face; my heart began to pound. I was certain that I smelled her perfume.

I took pride in being punctual, but I was late that day. My stage manager forgave me with a wink because it was the last day of the season. Many cast members had brought cameras, and there were continual flashes of light in the dressing rooms and backstage, followed by cheers and hugs. It was a festive occasion, and although we did have four shows to sold-out crowds to perform, the shows seemed to take a backseat to the emotions of the day.

I held it together until after the first show. I was resetting my costumes in the backstage area when I started to cry. The costume station next to mine belonged to Ray Kinman. He saw that I'd suddenly erupted with tears and grabbed me to hug and console me. "Shhhh, don't cry, don't cry," he said. He reassured me that this wouldn't be the end of all of us being friends and that he was confident that we'd both be back for Red Cast, which would be starting up again in the spring.

How was he to know that I was crying because my world had changed in the past twelve hours? How could he even imagine that I was scared and upset because I'd been sexual with a girl? I was crying because I was ashamed of the things I'd said to him about homosexuality. I cried so much into his shoulder that I messed up my eye makeup, most of which remained on his shirt. He gave me a kiss on the forehead and quipped in his best Southern diva voice, "Child, go fix yourself. You're a mess!"

Scared Straight

I didn't see Brenda that night. She called and left a couple of messages on the answering machine that was shared by everyone in the house. I didn't call her back. I just needed to be alone with my thoughts and figure out what in the world I was going to do.

I showed up at Sport Seasons the next morning for work. I knew that I'd be seeing Brenda and spending the whole day with her. The entire workday passed before I could get the courage to ask her if we could talk. In the meantime, I could feel her genuine concern for me and I sensed her discomfort that we still hadn't talked about what had happened. Just as we were closing the store, she asked me if I wanted to see her later that night. I told her I did because I wanted to talk to her about a couple of things.

There was really nowhere private for us to go except to my house, so we each headed that way in our own car. We went downstairs. I made sure every light in the basement living room was on.

I sat in a chair adjacent to the couch. "I'm not gay, Brenda. The other night was a mistake. I don't want to lose you as a friend, but what happened the other night can't happen again." She stared down at the rug on the floor and with the toe of her

Nike cross trainers attempted to straighten the fringe that was stitched to the edges. I watched her progress because I couldn't bear to look up at her. Every piece of the decorative maroon string was soon pointed perfectly in the same direction. She remained silent. I looked up and saw that her head was still hanging down. She was wearing a Sport Seasons T-shirt and a nice pair of tan pants. Her face was hidden from me. I saw that her pants, right at her knees, were wet with tears. Once I realized that she was crying, I got up and sat next to her on the couch. I put my arm around her and held on to her tightly. She finally lifted her head and said, "Okay, I'm sorry."

We talked a little bit more that night, but not much. We worked together during the next few days, and although it was a little awkward, I was hopeful that everything was going to be all right.

As the weeks went on, I was unable to resist spending my free time with her. She was gentle and sweet, and one of the prettiest girls I'd ever seen. I had asked her shortly after we first kissed if she'd ever done anything like that before. She told me no and it made me feel better. I began to hope that we were both just normal girls and that this was an isolated incident, not indicative of any reality that would manifest itself in my life. Thinking of it in those terms, that it was a first for both of us, made it easier for me for some reason. But our mutually imposed sanctions on being physical and sexual with one another didn't last long at all.

I worked throughout that fall at Sport Seasons and spent the rest of my time at Middle Tennessee State University. Most of my classes were in general studies, but I also took several political science courses. Brenda was a student there as well, and it was nice to have someone to share the burden of driving, as the campus was about forty-five minutes from Nashville. I was spending less and less time at home and seldom saw Laura-Grace and Gardnar. When I did go home, it made me nervous, because

Brenda was usually with me. I didn't want them to know what was going on between us, so I ended up staying with Brenda at her grandmother's apartment.

It made my stomach hurt to think about how I was living a dual existence. My belongings were in one place and I'd sleep in another. It was a very unsettling time in my life. When I was at Brenda's place, I longed to be back in my basement living area because that's where my keyboard was. Since I was a little girl of four years old, I'd played the piano nearly every day of my life. When I wrote songs, I leaned heavily on having a piano in front of me. Needless to say, I felt lost in so many ways and struggled to even recognize myself. I had no piano, and I was essentially living in two places and in a relationship with a girl. It started to scare me that I was choosing this unacceptable relationship over my music. I resented how this part of my life was forcing me to choose between my heart and my music. I felt so far away from my dreams at that time in my life. I just didn't see a way for my existence and my dreams to intersect. My entire life, I'd been able to imagine, in chronological and linear steps, how I would accomplish my goals. I had been able to envision Point A, Point B, Point C, and Point D, and then I'd just have to plan on how to connect the dots. This situation was different. These dots simply could not be connected.

I went home to be at my house for a while, to be with my piano. I played it all day long and through the night, and a new song began to take shape. Typically, once I had a new song written, I'd type out a page with the lyrics on it for future reference. There was an old blue electric typewriter that sat downstairs on a table just off the basement living area. I set my spiral notebook down next to it and began to scour the table for a fresh piece of typing paper. There was a piece of paper in the typewriter already, which was not unusual, as all of us in the house used that machine for schoolwork and other things. I looked at the paper already in the typewriter so I could determine which of my roommates was in the middle of a project.

I glanced down at the page. A single word was typed on the paper.

"Lesbian."

I couldn't imagine which one of my roommates had typed that. There were other people in and out of the house, but I speculated that whoever wrote it must have had enough knowledge about my comings and goings to know that I was spending a lot of time with Brenda. I pulled the page out of the machine hard, just the way my typing teacher in high school had told us not to do. I kept that piece of paper in my jewelry box for a long time. I eventually threw it away with a childish hope that the memory of it would go away too.

After the typewriter incident, I refused to allow Brenda to come over to the house. This was the time in my life when I started to learn how to hide on a whole new level. I had graduated from hiding my feelings of homosexuality to now having to hide my actions of homosexuality. It takes a lot of work to cover up an entire part of one's life, but desperate times call for desperate measures.

I needed to get my own apartment.

Brenda was unhappy living with her grandmother, so we decided to find a place together. Sometime in January 1990, Brenda and I moved into Priest Lake Apartments. We got a two-bedroom place, of course. I didn't know exactly how the situation would unfold, but somewhere in the back of my mind I suspected that we wouldn't stay together. The life of hiding was already proving to be stressful and frightening to me. I found myself pulling away from my parents and not calling them on the phone as often as I usually did. When I did speak to them, everything felt like a lie, even if they just asked, "What's been going on? What's new? Catch us up on things." My answers could pass, technically, for the truth—but it wasn't the truth and I knew it. I was telling lies by omission. It made me so sick that I developed a bleeding ulcer.

I did get hired back by Opryland to be in the Red Cast, the group of performers whose contracts were longer and a bit more secure. I threw myself into rehearsals, juggling my schedule with Sport Seasons, my classes, and hiding. My cast that year was composed mostly of the same folks from the Purple Cast, plus a few new faces. The three-week rehearsals that led up to opening day at the park were grueling. We were all excited because we knew we had an especially great cast and a well-written show to perform over the next nine months.

Opening day was always a big deal. Friends and family usually came out to watch our first couple of shows, and since I had no family that lived near, Brenda asked if she could come. I was nervous about her showing up. I didn't want anyone to ask me questions about who she was, but I wanted her to see my show. She did come to the debut of the show, and I was pleased that no one asked me much about her. She continued to come to the performances on occasion, and when she did, I worked extra hard at making sure my cast mates knew that I was ambivalent about her showing up. I tried to hide my smiles when I saw her. I did my best to avoid hugging her hello or good-bye.

Living with Brenda was relatively easy. She was a busy student at MTSU and a full-time employee of Sport Seasons. We didn't have great amounts of time together, but we did get into our routine as a couple. I was the leaseholder of the apartment, so she paid her rent and utilities to me each month. One evening while I was doing the bills, we started talking about things. I told her again that I didn't think I was gay. (I knew I was; I just didn't want to be.) I offered that she wasn't either. When I had asked her six months ago if she'd ever had any kind of sexual relationship with a girl before me, her answer had been "no." That night, while I was writing checks for the rent and the electric bill, I suggested that perhaps we were both normal girls and that this thing had nothing to do with homosexuality. We were attracted to each other . . . but we weren't gay.

Then she admitted that she had had a girlfriend before and that she lied to me because she didn't want to scare me off. She told me her story of two beautiful young girls in high school who fell in love. By the time the whole love affair unraveled, it had become ugly. She shared the sordid details of parents getting involved, fighting with one another about who had started the relationship, demands from a father shouting threats from a front porch daring one girl to take one more step toward his baby girl, and religious beliefs that Brenda and her girlfriend would burn in hell for what they were doing.

I was angry with Brenda for having lied to me and for telling me that I was the first girl she'd ever been attracted to, and I felt tricked. I'd constructed a theory inside my head that said if only I had known she'd been with a girl before, I wouldn't have gone through with being physical with her. I convinced myself that had she declared that she was a gay girl, I would've had my defenses up and would have been able to say no to this homosexual who was pursuing me. I know it was ridiculous, but I was scared and trying to do anything to identify myself as anything other than what I was—a homosexual. I knew deep down that I was lying to her too, though. I knew without a doubt that I was gay. But I continued to tell her otherwise.

I pulled back a little bit from her after she shared that story with me. I began to spend what little social time I had with my fellow performers from Opryland. Our cast decided to take a trip to the beach. I had never seen the ocean before and was excited to drive down to Gulf Shores, Alabama.

A dozen of us went and a few brought wives, girlfriends, boyfriends, or a pal. I didn't consider inviting Brenda, even though

I knew she would have loved to go. A couple of days before I left for our beach trip, Brenda asked if she could go. I said no.

The next morning, before I headed out to Opryland for a full day of shows, Brenda told me that she was so angry and hurt that she was going to do something and I'd be sorry. She told me that after I parked my car in the employee parking lot that day, she was going to find every car in the lot that belonged to my cast mates and put a flyer on each one saying that I was gay. "By this time tomorrow, all of your friends will know that you're gay." I begged her not to do it. She said it was too late, that she'd made up her mind.

One minute I was certain that she was just making idle threats and that she wouldn't do something like that; the next minute I was convinced that she would.

By the time I left the theater that night, I was preparing myself for the worst. Before the last show, I packed up my hair and makeup kit and all of my personal items so I could get a head start out of there. My plan was to reach the employee parking lot and scan it for cars with flyers under their windshield wipers. There were hundreds of cars in the lot, but I only needed to address sixteen of them. I ran to my car first and put my bags in the passenger seat. I remember specifically finding each of my cast mates' cars, one by one. No flyers. I saw a tram pull up to the lot and about eight of my friends got off and headed to their cars. I rushed to mine without being noticed, started it, and drove away. I was relieved but still upset. Although Brenda didn't follow through on her threat, she did inflict a type of revenge. Fear. She knew that I had a big red fear button and she pushed it.

I knew, at that point, that I would carefully take steps to distance myself from her.

From then on, I didn't sleep in her bedroom and she didn't sleep in mine. I felt like I was in a movie, a scared wife secretly planning her escape. She apologized for the threat and for putting me through such worry. She begged me for forgiveness, which I did honestly grant her. I couldn't forget what she had done, though, and I promised myself that I would never again put myself in that position. But things would get worse before they got better.

I asked Brenda to find another place to live and I assured her that she could take her time. A week or so after she said she would find a new living situation, I asked her how the search was going. She said that she had changed her mind, that she didn't want to move after all. She suggested that we live together as roommates and have no form of a relationship other than as friends. I knew she didn't mean that.

We began to argue and I ended up putting some of my things in a duffel bag. I was going to stay at Laura-Grace's until Brenda moved out. As I was almost to the door of the apartment, I heard her walk to the kitchen. She ran to where I was and got between the door and me. She'd grabbed the biggest knife in the kitchen. "You're not going anywhere," she said. She made me walk to the end of the hallway, back by the bedrooms, and sit with my back against the wall. We sat there for more than an hour.

I tried to calm her down, explaining to her that we needed to stop this situation; there was nothing good that could come of it. I wanted to call the police, but I wondered what I would tell them if I was even able to call. She got so angry with me that she began to threaten to out me again, to start calling my Opryland cast and to call my bosses at the park too. I stood up in the hallway and tried to walk away, but she grabbed me and pushed me against the wall. The drywall broke where my head hit it. It didn't knock me out, but it stunned me. I was terrified and I began to cry.

It was then that she realized how out of control she was. She just slid to the floor and cried. I wanted to console her, but I didn't. I picked up my duffel bag, walked out the door, and stayed away until she moved out. Within a week I was back in my apartment, alone.

After that I focused on my music. I had my keyboard with me, and I wrote songs anytime I could. During the day, I worked at Opryland and Sport Seasons, mostly at a new store location far from Brenda. I went to my classes at MTSU and spent time trying to get to know songwriters on Nashville's famed Music Row.

Occasionally I did see Brenda. Once, I even went over to her new apartment. I felt it was important to try and stay friendly with her, and I honestly did miss her friendship. A month after our breakup, she started to see another girl; I was relieved.

"Dear God, please don't let me be gay," I would say in the quiet of my apartment. "I promise to be a good person. I promise not to lie. I promise not to steal. I promise to always believe in you. I promise to do all the things you ask me to do. Please take it away. In your name I pray. Amen."

A few months later, a man asked me out to dinner and a movie. He was nice, handsome, and had a good job. We ate dinners, watched movies, and spent time together for a few months. I felt nothing—absolutely nothing.

For the next three years, I was able to deny myself the affection I craved. From time to time, I dated men, but those relationships were short-lived and faded away.

My First Recording Contract, 1993

When Harold Shedd signed me to my first record contract, in 1993, I was naively adamant about certain things. I recall sitting in his office at Mercury Records and discussing my vision of what kind of artist I wanted to be. I was not kidding when I told him that I had no interest in being a video babe. I told him that I wanted to be recognized in country music for my music and that I didn't want teams of stylists being assigned to me to fix me up and make me fashionable. While I had always enjoyed my femininity, I'd never had a great interest in getting dolled up. I knew, to some extent, that I'd have to be aware of my image, but I didn't want it to be something that eclipsed what I believed to be my art.

Harold told me that he respected my position in the matter and that he had full intentions of presenting me as a serious musician, but that he couldn't be held responsible if anyone thought I might be pretty to look at. I was taking myself far too seriously and quickly learned that I should use all of the tools I possessed to help me along the way.

It was a new era in country music. Videos were becoming a common part of the promotion of an artist's music. Many people acknowledged this and attributed the explosion to Garth

Brooks's phenomenal success at that time. Before Garth's emergence in country music there were six or seven major country labels out of Nashville. With so much subsequent worldwide attention on country music, major record labels began branching out. There were new divisions, sister labels, and imprint labels. Before long, Nashville's Music Row would be overflowing with new buildings to house new labels. These labels were signing new artists left and right, and I was one of them. Country music fans weren't buying only Garth's records. They would be attracted to the genre because of their love for Garth, but once they decided to give country music a chance, they started buying records from a lot of other artists. Money was flowing in Music City.

Julia

I met the love of my life on April Fool's Day, 1993. She was working in the music industry, and shortly after I was signed to Mercury Records our paths crossed. She was beautiful, interesting, and funny, and it didn't take long for me to realize that I was falling for her. At the time, I was dating a man called Chris. I broke up with him soon after meeting Julia; I knew where my heart was headed. She was recovering from a recent breakup with a longtime boyfriend, but I sensed that the biggest part of her suffering came more from the blow to her ego than from missing him. Nevertheless, we were both single and had no one to answer to but ourselves.

We spent all of our free time together, but many months went by before we discussed what we were feeling. When she asked me if I'd ever before had feelings for a woman, I lied. Just like Brenda had lied to me.

Once we did discuss it, we agreed that we shouldn't act on our attraction; neither one of us thought it was acceptable to be in a gay relationship. She had been raised Catholic, and although I knew very well that my natural instincts were to be with a woman, I just didn't want it. It was an exciting time in my life. I was writing and recording my first album and all those years of struggle were finally starting to pay off. I had money in my pocket for meals and could pay my rent with no worry. My life was beginning to take the shape I'd imagined, and falling in love with Julia would complicate things. I was a public person and had to navigate those risky waters, and because she was in the country music industry too, we were very well aware that if we were to be together we'd have to hide.

I think I fell in love with her before our first kiss, but once we began to be sexual with each other, our connection strengthened. Any act of togetherness felt intimate, whether it was holding hands, falling asleep, or waking up together. I knew during those times that if I were asked to make a choice in my lifetime to have only those few acts with her versus a thousand sexual interactions with a man, I would choose hand-holding with Julia.

I was more willing to allow myself to be with her than she was with me during those first few months of our relationship. Every couple of weeks, she'd suggest that we should just be friends. When she made those declarations, I expressed my feelings to the contrary but promised that I'd try to respect her position. A day or two later, she'd break down and say that she'd changed her mind because she didn't think she could bear to be without me.

We'd been in a good place for a couple of months, without the usual every-other-day meltdown, when she called me on the phone one Friday afternoon. I assumed that she was calling to let me know what time she thought she'd be through with work that evening so we could meet up. At that point in my career, because I was recording and I wasn't touring, I had my weekends to myself. I enjoyed every minute of that time with Julia.

I answered the phone and I was taken aback by what she told me.

"Do you know that guy Phillip? He's a singer-songwriter here in town."

"I've heard of him, but I don't know him. Why?"

"I'm thinking of going on a date with him tonight."

I listened, trying not to cry, and asked her why she was telling me this. She wanted to let me know before she did it. She called me again within an hour and asked if I wanted to go with them. Even though I knew it was odd for her to invite me, and more bizarre for me to go, I said yes.

I went with Julia and Phillip on their first date and whether I wanted to or not, I liked him instantly. We ate dinner, then found a pool hall where I uncharacteristically drank too much beer. I felt so bad the next morning, physically and emotionally.

Julia told me that they had spent the weekend together and that he was crazy about her. She said that he was funny and she liked how much he liked her. She simply seemed pleased that he was a nice, fun guy. She went on to say that she had confided in him that she and I loved each other but that she wanted to have a normal life. He told her that her relationship with me was fine with him, and he appreciated the complex person that she was. I'm not sure if he was telling her that he was okay with her loving me or if he was saying that it was okay for us to actually "be together." Nevertheless, it was understood that she and I had a special relationship.

Julia and Phillip spent the next few months together. I pulled back, not because I wasn't drawn to her but because I found the situation confusing and a bit hopeless. We did try to hang out together now and again. I'd been going out on dates with a guy named Daniel in hopes of being granted a miracle of my own, that I'd fall in love with a man. I didn't fall in love with Daniel. What I ended up doing was leaving him perplexed and hurt by my detached behavior.

Julia, Phillip, Daniel, and I even spent time together. Daniel was quite the host, and he decided to have a barbecue at his house one Saturday afternoon. He invited about thirty people to visit, eat, drink, and be merry on his back porch. I was on the road promoting my first single, but was scheduled to fly back to

Nashville on Saturday around noon. I got home from the airport, got myself ready, and drove over to Daniel's house on Belmont Boulevard for the gathering. Even though the skies threatened to open up, there were lots of people there, mostly music industry folks.

I found Daniel in the kitchen whipping up an impressive culinary concoction. He asked me to announce to everyone on the front porch that the beer and food were on the back porch. On the way, I ran into Phillip. We hugged, he asked me how the tour was going, and if I'd heard. "Heard what?" I said. He had proposed to Julia that morning and she'd said yes. I turned and walked down the steps of Daniel's front porch, onto the street, and like a zombie, began to walk up Belmont Boulevard. It started to pour down rain and it seemed fitting.

I'd walked half a mile or so when I noticed Phillip's little blue truck pulling up in the street next to me. Julia was seated on the passenger side and she rolled down the manual crank window, asking me to get in, to get out of the rain. I said no and kept walking. She asked if I was sure and, without ever once looking her way, I said, "Yes, I'm sure." My car was back at Daniel's and I didn't even have my purse, but I walked for a long time. Eventually, I made my way back to Daniel's house. All of the guests were in the backyard. I walked in unnoticed, grabbed my purse, got in my car, and left.

Julia called the next day and left a voice mail message saying that she was sorry she didn't tell me before Phillip did, but that she just wanted to have a normal life and she wished I'd just understand. The next day, I called her back at work. I knew that if I called her there, she wouldn't be able to talk for more than a minute or two. I lied, telling her that I completely understood, then quickly got off the phone.

Honestly, what did I expect her to do? Did I think that she and I could really survive, with any quality of life, in Nashville, Tennessee? I was a brand-new artist on Mercury/PolyGram

Records; they were pumping millions of dollars into my career. How could I risk ruining my chances of making it as a successful country music artist? I was just getting started. I continued to hope that I'd be able to look back one day on those confusing times and reference them as a "phase" that I went through. I wanted to be normal too and tried to convince myself that this was the best thing for us.

Julia and Phillip had a short engagement. In the weeks leading up to their wedding, I spent a minimal amount of time with her. We talked on the phone and shared a few meals together. I was on the road most of the time and was thankful for the distraction. I called her at her office on a Monday morning to say hello. She asked me how my weekend had been. I filled her in on the details of promoting my record and asked her what she'd done over the weekend. She said, "Oh, Phillip and I got married."

I gave a halfhearted wish of congratulations and got off the phone. I was angry with her for going through with it, but I was also able to recognize that her marrying Phillip was a desperate Hail Mary heaved in the direction of "normal." I continued to focus on my career and was as busy as I wanted to be. Considering that the woman I loved had just gotten married to someone else, staying busy was the only thing I could do.

The days that I wasn't on the road touring, doing promotion for my record, or doing a photo shoot, I was writing songs back in Nashville at my office on Music Row. I was co-writing with Harlan Howard, Whitey Shafer, and Bobby Braddock, among others. I was, as they say in the South, "walking in high cotton." When I missed Julia, I'd tell myself to get over it and be thankful for the other things that were going so well for me.

I didn't really want to hear the details of their newlywed life, so I stayed away. On occasion, I would accept their invitation to go out to dinner or to just spend time at their apartment for a couple of hours. I was doing my best to tell myself that if I couldn't love Julia as my girlfriend, I'd rather have her in my life as a friend. Soon they announced to me that they were buying a house, and the three of us piled into Phillip's truck and went to look at it.

I wanted to be happy for them, but I felt an incredible amount of hurt. I wondered if she was hoping that being with him, married for all of Music Row to see, would replace me. I wondered if the amenities of that marriage would be enough for her. A brand-new house, the new Chihuahua puppy they'd just bought together, the title of "Mrs.," and a joint checking account—did all of that add up to be as good as or better than having me?

Suffering that kind of rejection was overwhelming. I was forced to rationalize. The only reason I survived those particular months was because my brain kicked into high gear and continued to remind me of my reality. I was an up-and-coming country music singer, living in Nashville, Tennessee, and there had never been an openly gay country music star. I knew that I could not—I would not—be the first.

Being on the road during the release of my first album was an exhilarating experience that filled some of the voids I felt in my life. I took it in and allowed myself to be distracted by my new routines. I missed Julia every day. I wrote notes to her in my hotel rooms that I never sent. I had conversations with her in my head and sometimes spoke my words out loud when I could find private moments. As tormented as I was personally, it was impossible to deny the fact that my job was a blast. Sometimes I'd lie in my bunk as the tour bus rolled down the road and take inventory of all that I was enjoying. I had a contract with a major record label, a song on the radio, a music video on TV, my own tour bus, my own six-piece band and four-man crew, people to dress me, a hair and makeup artist, and more fans than I could count in a lifetime. I began to look at all of the positives as an emotional consolation prize. I guessed that if there were other public people like me who were gay and hiding, they probably felt just like I did. I'm sure they too hoped and prayed that career achievements and success would be enough to sustain their happiness.

With George Brett, after I sang the National Anthem at a Kansas City Royals season opener in 2005.

A Dream Come True

In the spring of 1995, I was nominated for the Top New Female Vocalist award by the Academy of Country Music. The award show would air live on national television from Los Angeles. I was beside myself with excitement that even though I hadn't scored that big hit record yet, the Academy (made up of people in the industry) had nominated me. My record label and my manager at the time told me, "We're a long shot," and I said, "That's okay. I'm just glad that my family will get to see me on the show!" That was true. I was happy to be included.

I'd been in Los Angeles doing press for several days, and finally the moment had come. During the broadcast, there was a television commercial break, and the performers in the audience were milling around, talking to one another. As the show went to the break, the announcer said, "Coming up next, the Top New Female Vocalist award!" Directly across the aisle, seated to my left, was Barbara Mandrell. I don't know a female country singer out there today who hasn't been influenced by her. I'd known Barbara since 1990 and had always felt fortunate to hear her words of wisdom. She motioned for me to come to her, so I did. I knelt down by her seat and she took my hand and held it with both of hers. The first thing she said was, "Your hands are freezing, little girl!" Then she said, "Remember exactly how this feels

Kenny Chesney and I met in 1993. For a while we had the same manager and producer. We spent time together touring, writing songs, and just being friends. This photograph was taken the night I won my Academy of Country Music Award in 1995.

Toby Keith and me at the BMI Awards in 2005. We were each signed to Mercury Records but ended up being shuffled around under the PolyGram umbrella to be the flagship artists for Polydor Records. He was one of the performers who presented me with my ACM Award onstage.

right now." I nodded my head yes. "It will never get more exciting than this very moment, your first nomination."

The presenters walked onstage, read the names of the nominees, then opened the envelope. "And the winner for the Top New Female Vocalist is . . ."

Everything turned to slow motion. I heard my name being called. I still have no memory of how I made it up to the podium. I had not prepared a speech for that night, but I'd been rehearsing one since I was a little girl, and the right words came out. Barbara Mandrell's advice to me allowed me to absorb what was happening. As I looked out at the audience and said my thank-you's, I received proud smiles and thumbs-up from the biggest names in country music. It was one of the greatest moments of my career.

The Thin Line

L ate one night I was at my apartment packing for a tour in Japan—months after I'd been given my ACM—when the phone rang. It was Aunt Char calling to tell me to fly safely the following day and to ask me what I'd think if my parents were to get divorced.

"What?" I asked. "Are you serious?"

"It might be lookin' that way, kiddo."

She wasn't able to shed much light on the matter and, frankly, I don't recall that I had many questions for her. I can't even say that I was upset about the possibility that my mom and dad might be splitting up, but I do know I was surprised. They'd always seemed bound and determined to stay together despite their obvious mutual misery. Even I at a very young age, perhaps in my early teens, knew that they needed to get professional help, call the whole thing off, or both.

I climbed aboard my international flight the next day and confided my parents' potential break-up to my drummer, Preston, who'd been as close to me as any family member. He was concerned, and did his best to provide comfort during that trip. Preston had been around my folks a good amount of time, and he shared my sentiment about the situation, that it wasn't so much sad as it was weird. Whatever warts and dysfunction my parents' marriage may have had, they just seemed to have a style and a visible *that makes sense* to their relationship. People, including me (especially after I became a young adult), enjoyed being around them. Most of the time, they were funny and clever.

As I watched my bandmates slip into sleep at thirty-eight-thousand feet, I began to dissect what had happened in the recent twenty-four hours of my life. I wondered if Aunt Char had called to tip me off, or if she had called to deliver a message sent by one or both of my parents. If it had been the latter, I thought, that would be bizarre, because my mother and I had always been so close, even into my adulthood. Why wouldn't she tell me herself?

I was my mother's youngest child, her baby, and yes, I think she favored me. Perhaps I benefited, in age-old fashion, by being the lucky last in the birth order. When chores were finished, spankings had been administered to each of us, and homework was complete—from even the young age of five, I could usually be found spending time with my mom. We'd listen to records, read liner notes in albums. I'd help her re-thread the bobbin on her old Singer sewing machine, we'd play Gin Rummy, and we'd talk about things—big and small.

I wouldn't say we were friends or buddies, but I liked my mom. She was the mother, and I was the child—that was evident.

When I was very young, perhaps even until junior high school, I adored my mom and thought that she was the wisest woman on earth. I have no idea if this is an unusual notion for a kid or not. She was my mother: she fed me, she taught me to read and write, and she showed me how to put an unwilling worm on my hook and pull a catfish out of a low-water creek. How could I *not* think she was all-knowing?

But something ran parallel to that adoration for my mother, and that was fear.

Of course, I had fear of both of my parents—in different measure, for different reasons. My dad gave spankings, as we called them, which sometimes left our legs covered in welts. The asterisk to that particular fear of my father is that my mother was always (as I recall) the one to instruct my dad to dole out the spankings. From my adult perspective, I can see that my dad was still unable to parent his children, and if it were left up to him, I think he'd have taken the easier route and never punished us. The other fear I had of my dad was the fear I assumed on my mom's behalf. When my dad would be angry with my mother (in my younger years, alcohol made him go nuclear), I became frightened of him—for her. I knew during their screaming matches, which sometimes turned physical, that my dad was not going to hit or harm *me,* yet I took on tremendous amounts of fear. I don't recall my mom hitting me outside the customary 1970s swatting of the child's backside with a wooden spoon, fly-swatter, or hand; it was usually three or four staccato quarter-note swats accompanied by a spoken-word lyric: "I. Said. Stop. That." Which I did. And it barely hurt. The fear I had for my mother was much more frightening, and each time that fear would come to pass, it never left a mark on my body.

Even as a tiny girl, the biggest fear I had of my mother was that of not having her approval and affection. When my mother assigned household tasks for me to do, I executed them as perfectly as I could. A well-cleaned bathtub or a symmetrically folded bedsheet would, on occasion, earn me high marks.

"Did I get that really clean, Mom?" "That's pretty good how all those cans of soup are lined up the way you like 'em, huh?"

"Yes, Squirrelly, you did a good job." She might say, punctuating her praise with the slightly crooked smile she got from my grandfather and passed down to me.

There were times when I just plainly and simply needed affection. I have so many memories of failed attempts to get hugs, but one memory has always represented the entire library of denial.

I must've been about five years old. Chris and Jeny were at school, and it's likely that I was upset because I wanted to be there too. I sat in the big bay window of the dining room playing with the homemade Raggedy Ann doll my mom had recently made for me. She did thoughtful things like that for all three of us, but those acts were sporadic and never made much sense to me. I remember thinking that even though the shades of red on my doll didn't quite look like those on the real Raggedy Ann doll, otherwise my doll did look a lot like the real thing. My mother was talking on the kitchen telephone. I waited until I heard the clunk of the receiver as it rattled back into place, and I dragged my stocking feet over hardwood then linoleum to get to her. She was standing in the middle of the room and just as I hooked my arm around the top of her good knee and pressed my right temple to her outer thigh, she reached down and pried me off of her.

"No," she said. "I hurt."

I wouldn't realize until I was much older that my mother suffered every day from chronic pain, as a result of her polio and from the dozen or so surgeries performed on her legs.

I adored her so much when I was young, and my love for her has grown up in the ways that *I* have grown up. I have convinced myself that I haven't completely lost her—that we're still hanging on by a thread. If I tell her I'm gay, I worry that a definitive laser beam of disgust and rejection will zap that thread in two, with such velocity that there won't even be smoke or fire, no evidence of a burn—just a cold, freezing cut that will send me spiraling down, looking up at her like I did when I was five years old.

We Found a Way

Not long into Julia and Phillip's marriage, shortly after I'd been signed to MCA Records, Julia and I rekindled our relationship. She wasn't sorry that she had married him, and in fact I wasn't sorry either. The three of us spent a lot of time together, and over the years I came to consider Phillip as close as a family member. I wouldn't say that they had an open marriage, because my understanding of that type of relationship is that the married couple continues to be intimate. Along those lines, we weren't what they call "swingers" either. My relationship was with Julia and Julia only. They seemed to be happy living in the same house, being the best of friends, and spending time together when they chose. She and I did everything together. We took vacations, often to remote cabins located in state parks. We loved to hike and explore together, but we also appreciated the privacy that we could find in a little log cabin in the woods. Phillip always encouraged our time together, and when we'd take off on a trip or if I were around, he'd say, "Yay, C's here. I can go play now!"

Mostly, he was joking when he'd say that, but there was a part of him that wasn't. He often said that Julia was simply happier when I was there. He claimed that the weekends when I was on the road were tough on him because she missed me so much.

I bought a house about five miles from their house, so it was easy for us to be together. On nights when I was home in Nashville, we'd sleep either at her house or at mine. We had a routine that worked for us, and the effort it took to make it happen was worth it to both of us. I was actually glad on so many occasions that Julia was married, because it provided us with a certain cover under which we could hide. Her marriage to Phillip was never part of a scheme to camouflage the existence of our relationship, but it certainly added an element of disguise for which I was thankful.

All-American Girl

I'm called a hard worker. I think I'm known as a nice person, too—a lady, with good manners. This is important to me, to be ladylike. I've been amazed at some of the behaviors of women in the entertainment industry, on all levels.

There are women in every position of the entertainment business, and I am aware that this didn't come about easily. I know that there were females who carved a path for the rest of us to get to do what we do, and it is a little easier on each passing generation of women. These women who were pioneers were forced to prove themselves in a man's world.

I'm not suggesting that sexism and inequality don't still exist in the country music industry; they are very much alive, but some progress has been made. I suppose that early on, when women were first starting to have solo careers and were actually working behind the scenes in the entertainment world, they had to play tough. I've heard legendary stories over the years about women and how they were faced with a decision of how to approach their careers. One path was to use their sexuality to advance their position. Even when they were simply going along with it, they were perpetuating an archaic role for women. I do understand that in many cases, had these women bucked the system, they would have been fired or somehow squeezed out.

Another way was to toughen up, be one of the boys, and play

Loretta Lynn is the greatest influence on my music, and I still get nervous when I'm in her presence. She called me personally to invite me to a party celebrating her Grammy nomination for the Jack White–produced album Van Lear Rose *in 2004.*

When I was growing up, Buck Owens was one of my musical heroes. Once I got to know him on a personal level, he became an even greater hero. We were very good friends. I learned so much from him, not only about music but about the business. 1996.

a macho game, and that is still happening today. I knew all of this early on in my career and was confused as to how I would fit in. I wouldn't take that path as a straight woman and I didn't do it as a gay woman. It wasn't an issue of sexuality for me. It was not in my personality to play tough, act macho, and be one of the boys in that regard.

I don't lead with sex, hetero or homo. I don't swear in public, seldom in front of men. I don't tell off-color jokes in mixed company, and if an off-color joke is being told in my presence, I try to slip away. I just remove myself from the situation. I have found in my career that one sets boundaries early on to one's peers and associates. I guess I let people know in the first couple of years of my career who I was and how I wanted to be treated. I wanted to be treated with respect, and I wanted to be treated like a lady. I have seen many females in my business try to take a shortcut to fit in or to become successful, either by becoming a sex object or by taking on the role of "one of the boys" only to later feel frustration that they weren't being shown respect as women. I'm not a tough girl. I have manners, I am ladylike, and I am gay.

I'm known as a good American. I hear it so often, but I wonder what it means.

I began spending time with people in the military and veterans very early in my life. My grandfather Harold Henry had been a sergeant in the Second World War. After I declared to him at a young age that I had dreams of performing country music, he encouraged me to go play for guys at the VA hospital. From about age nine, I would travel once a month with Wellsville's local American Legion members up to the VA in the city. I had no fear or hesitation in getting to know these old men and hearing their stories of service and war, which at times would be very tragic. There were stories that were carefree as well, detailing accounts of travel to exotic destinations and of people who sounded nothing like the people I knew. All of that led me to develop a deep appreciation and understanding of what they'd done for our country, not to mention giving me a glimmer of comprehension of how big the world really was.

Furthering my associations with the military, once I began to play the trumpet in the junior high school band, I gladly took on the duty of being the official bugler for the American Legion. During Memorial Day programs in my school or in my town, I would be the one to play taps. I also took my trumpet to military funerals and burial services. I would stand in the distance and play as the family members of the deceased veteran were given an American flag perfectly folded into a triangle. The ceremony is sacred and emotional, and in a perfect world every veteran would have a live bugler at his or her burial service. Taps is a powerful melody, and there is nothing like that sorrowful tune as it cries out of a live brass instrument. I was the bugler from seventh grade until the day I packed my car and headed to Nashville. My grandfather had asked me during my time as the bugler if he could count on me to play taps for him when that day should come. He died a little more than a year after I moved to Tennessee. Grandpa and Grandma had just spent a week with me in Nashville and had seen me perform live, for the first time in my life, on the Grand Ole Opry stage. I traveled back to Kansas with my trumpet. It was the last time I ever played taps.

I started going overseas to entertain the troops in the mid-1990s. My first international trip was not military in nature, though. It was a huge outdoor country music festival in Japan. I was a backup singer in Porter Wagoner's band, and every show he'd invite me up to center stage to sing a few songs on my own and to perform a duet with him. Porter, his band, and I traveled to Kumamoto, Japan, and I was instantly enamored of the experience of international travel.

The show was at the base of Mount Fuji, and there were about forty thousand people in attendance. It was the day of my twenty-first birthday, and at one point the host of the show, Charlie Nagatani, led the enormous crowd of Japanese country music fans in singing "Happy Birthday" to me.

The promoter of that show was a woman by the name of Judy

Seale. I found her to be very good at her job, and even though I was just a lowly background singer for Porter, she treated me with a great deal of respect and friendliness. She had multiple acts on the show and still had the graciousness to be so nice to me. The Forester Sisters, the Texas Tornados, Porter Wagoner, and all of us were in for a treat, because this Japanese crowd was more excited than any crowd I'd ever witnessed. I couldn't believe how the locals knew every word to every song sung on the show, even though they really didn't understand the meaning of the words.

Judy had tried to tell me that this would be the case, and she was right; the crowd was insanely into country music. On that first trip to Japan, I soaked up the foreign culture with great appreciation and wonder. In the years that followed, Judy would become one of my dearest friends and we'd travel the world together.

Over the next couple of years, I not only toured all over the United States, but I saw Switzerland, Norway, Canada, the Netherlands, Germany, Brazil, and England. I couldn't get enough. I was fascinated with my reality. I still could not believe that I could be so far away from my small Kansas town, doing exactly what I'd dreamed of doing since I was a little girl. The thing was, when I imagined my life as a country music star, I envisioned traveling across the United States. I don't think that I ever visualized world travel. I felt as though I was in a movie that didn't have to have an end.

There is something so thrilling about flying halfway around the world and singing to people who actually know your songs and sing them back to you. Yes, I enjoyed the shows, but my favorite part of international travel was experiencing the way other people lived. Seeing what they saw, eating their cuisine, although many times I wasn't sure what I was looking at and I was tentative about what I was putting in my mouth—it was always an adventure.

Once I landed at my destination, there would be a van ride, bus ride, or car ride to the town where the show was to be. These rides would profoundly affect me—I was slowly coming to understand that the rest of the world did not live like we do in the United States. I'd always heard that—that we were privileged to be Americans. Yes, it was true that I grew up with very little by American standards, but I was seeing people and places on other continents that didn't have it nearly as good as I'd had it.

Everything I saw was different—the architecture, the terrain, the cars, the trees, the grass—sometimes the only things I recognized were the sky, the moon, and the sun. It made me feel so alive. I knew it had been out there, a different and bigger world. And during those moments in cars and on buses, I thanked God for giving me my ticket to see the world. Music, sweet music.

About a year into my touring, my agent mentioned to me that a promoter had contacted him about some international concerts. When he said that the promoter's name was Judy Seale, I smiled and told him that Judy was an old friend whom I'd met years before on a show in Japan. The tour dates worked out, and during that trip Judy and I realized that we shared a respect for people who serve in the military. She asked me if I wanted to go overseas and do shows just for the troops sometime, to say thank you.

My first trip overseas to perform for the military was to South Korea. It was a ten-day trip. I had had a marginal knowledge about the ways of the military, as most Americans do, but I got a crash course on protocol and procedure in those first ten days. I remember thinking that I was well suited for it, this military life. My folks had run our household much like a little boot camp anyway, so this first trip to Korea wasn't a shock.

We didn't even allow ourselves time to recognize the jet lag.

Judy talked us through some of her tricks to avoid fatigue before we got on that long flight. She had suggestions about how much water to drink on the flight, what to eat and not eat, when to sleep on the plane and when to force yourself to stay awake. She is the most traveled human being I know, and if anyone has tricks, it's Judy.

We were welcomed at Incheon Airport in Seoul by no fewer than a dozen military escorts. They were professional, friendly, informed, and impressive in their skill at getting us safely and happily from Point A to Point B. When touring for the troops, we often slept on the bases, and the base quarters were just fine with us. I thought it was really cute how our sharply dressed and well-mannered escorts continued to apologize that the accommodations they'd arranged might not be up to our standards because we must be so used to fancy hotels and such. I tried to explain to them that we spent most of our time crammed into a tour bus and that we were used to existing with very little glamour at all.

We all slept just a couple of hours, then headed off for the day. Judy told us to take everything we would need, since we wouldn't be returning for almost twenty-four hours. The plan was to go to several different locations during the day and end up at the venue for the show that night. I must've signed autographs in five different places that day. We visited the men way out in the field who were doing training missions and wouldn't be able to attend the show.

The shows for the troops are always high-energy events, both from the stage and from the audience. Much of the crowd knows me or knows my music, but there are always folks who have never heard of my songs who come out to the show anyway. They are just so happy that anyone would travel all that way to sing for them. After the show, as on any and all Judy Seale military dates, the artist signs autographs and meets people until the last person is gone. Although this policy can be painful and almost impossible at times, it is the reason why I love to play for the troops—having the opportunity to talk to them. And just as important as that, it's why I love to do military shows with Judy. She will not settle for the troops' getting less than everything the artist has to offer. I've known her to scold some of the biggest stars in music today if they whine about not wanting to endure the autograph sessions. "Yes, I know it's hard," she'll say. "You think their jobs aren't hard? Now get your Sharpie and go sign."

That first day of the South Korea tour proved to be as long and busy as Judy had warned us it would be, lasting about twenty hours. When we finally made it back to the barracks, we slept another couple of hours, then got up and did it all over again, for seven more days.

We flew in helicopters to some of the most faraway camps to see the troops who seldom got a visit. On many of those days, there weren't adequate situations to set up a stage to have a show, so we'd take a couple of guitars and wing it. My drummer, Preston, played many a show without a drum. He'd bring his drumsticks and he'd figure out once we got to where we were going what exactly would be his makeshift drum for that show— a cardboard box, a five-gallon bucket, a table, or a board. He was always a trouper.

One of my favorite shows for the military took place in the DMZ, that narrow strip of land that separates North Korea and South Korea. It is a highly policed zone that is heavily guarded by both sides. The tension up there on that ever-so-volatile little piece of the earth was noticeable to us. Once we got on post, we could tell that the guys who were stationed there were really ready to have a good time. They needed a break. We played in the corner of the dining facility in the middle of the day with no equipment and no stage. There was a young soldier who knew my songs and had brought his harmonica to the show in hopes that we might allow him to get up and play with us. I invited him up. The band and I anticipated that he'd stumble through the song and that the crowd would give him an obligatory round of applause for having the courage to sit in with us. Much to our surprise, he could play, and he lifted up the entire performance. Over the years he has popped up in the crowd when we've played at different military installations around the world—always with the harp in his pocket, and he always joins us onstage.

"But Didn't She Date
What's-His-Name?"

I never dated a man for show. Some people in entertainment do that—date someone to throw people off track so others won't know they're gay. It's been going on for years in Hollywood. I have dated men but never for the purpose of fooling anyone.

In the fall of 1998, Julia and I were trying to figure out a way to exist. We were deeply in love, but the reality of our being together was scary and seemed impossible. She was married to Phillip, and they had carved out a life that was routine but separate. We tried on many occasions to quit one another—we'd usually try to go "cold turkey." It was torture knowing that our objective was simply to get through the day without communicating. We'd decided that it would be difficult at first, but we thought that as the days, weeks, and months passed, we surely wouldn't miss one another quite so badly. I thought that it would get easier—but it didn't for me.

I didn't know how she was handling it, because we weren't in contact, so I assumed that she was fine with this new situation and was moving on with her life. My heart was shattered, but I did my best to keep my chin up and think of ways to move on with mine as well.

I'd known Vince Gill for a couple of years and had been

thrilled to have him sing on my first MCA album. Tony Brown was my producer at the time, and since he and Vince were best friends, Tony called him to sing on my project. When the time came around to record my next album, I called Vince and asked him if he'd share his talents yet again.

Vince and I were both MCA artists, so there had been times when we'd be corralled at the same event and we'd end up having easy conversation between us.

Both of us were working at the Sound Stage Studio on Music Row in the fall of 1998. We were just down the hall from each other and ended up in the lounge talking and I found him to be charming and quite likable, as does the rest of the world. Vince has been one of Nashville's most beloved stars for decades, and anyone who ever gets the chance to be around him just falls in love with him.

He'd recently been through a very public divorce and was currently being run through the rumor mill about his relationship with Amy Grant, another revered artist in Nashville's music community. Vince and Amy had been close friends for years, and it was highly speculated that they were in love. I remember thinking if Vince and Amy were in love, it made sense to me.

Vince and I began spending private time together soon after our studio chats. We had a lot in common, and in the years after our relationship I realized that we shared one bonding similarity: we were both lonely for, and in love with, someone else. At that time neither one of us was able to be with our one true love, so we allowed ourselves to find comfort in each other.

Early in my relationship with Vince, I understood that his heart would never belong to me. To some degree, that was a relief because it assured me that I wouldn't end up hurting him. Amy knew that Vince and I were spending a lot of our time together, but when I'd see her, she was always kind to me anyway.

I cared for Vince and while we were seeing each other, I imagined what my life would be like if we continued our relationship.

*With Vince Gill, having fun at a charity
sporting event in 2005.*

Vince isn't into the party scene. He lives well below his means and doesn't require a group of people around him at all times to baby him. I liked these things about him, and I assume he liked the same qualities in me. We looked pretty good on paper.

We toured together too, and I found him to be the exact same guy on the road as he was in Nashville. I adored him, and we shared a special relationship during critical times in each of our lives. I am still friendly with Vince, and Amy too. They are two of the finest people I've ever known.

"Single White Female"

The day we recorded a song called "Single White Female," we all knew that we'd done something special. My producers—Tony, Buddy Cannon, and Norro Wilson—were telling me, with great confidence, that we had just cut a hit. If anybody knew hits, it was these three guys, as they had been responsible for producing many successful records in country music that spanned the decades.

Norro Wilson, me, and Buddy Cannon in 1999. Great producers—greater men.

"Single White Female" was the title track of what would come to be my fourth album. I'd had my first Top 10 with my previous MCA album, but we stumbled with the follow-up singles from that project. I needed a hit and I needed it badly.

I was one of the fortunate few to be in such a great position—signed to, at that time, the most successful record label in Nashville. MCA Records signed me after I'd made two albums for PolyGram that didn't do so well. Just getting one record contract in one's lifetime is an amazing feat, but to have another major label sign you to a second contract with no track record of success is unusual.

I'm pretty sure that there was some luck involved in why I was still getting chances with Nashville and with country radio, despite my low-charting first six singles during my PolyGram days. That said, I believe in the old saying "Luck is where opportunity and preparation collide." I worked, I toured, and I wrote. I did everything asked of me by the label, the publicists, and the managers.

It's understandable behavior for an artist to become frustrated with a record label when the artist's records seem to struggle on the charts—that's a typical response. Some artists get angry or upset and they shut down. When one goes through the process of landing a contract, pouring one's heart out in songwriting, making the album, then doing the promotional tour to get ready to release the record, only to have the label tell you that the first single has bombed—well, that is a devastating blow.

When it happened to me, when I could see that my first couple of singles were failing, I had a choice to make. I could do the usual get-mad-at-the-label-and-refuse-to-do-anything-that-they-ask-me-to-do, or I could do the unusual do-anything-and-everything-asked-of-me. I chose the unusual. I recall that when my label, managers, and publicists could see that this was how I was going to handle myself, they were surprised. They were happy, of course, because they had all been in the business longer than I had and they knew the value of a work ethic like mine. I think that many of them decided, "Hey, this gal has what it takes to really make it in this industry." I soon realized the people with whom I was working were treating me differently—with even greater respect and a new sense of resolve.

My team of people started to become emotionally invested in my career. I had once been a project that they were assigned to work, and now I was an artist about whom they were passionate. I was becoming known in Nashville and in country radio as one of the hardest-working new artists around. Mind you, the work that was being asked of me was not that difficult—they weren't asking me to throw hay bales up on the back of a flatbed trailer; they weren't asking me to pour and finish concrete. It was not hard labor, for the most part. They were asking me to come in and sign five hundred posters at once—big deal. Or they were asking me to go on the road for weeks, with little time to sleep, and do shows for radio and sign autographs at Wal-Mart for hours on end for free. So what? I'd been doing that for years, working that hard for very little or no money. This was not a problem for me. I loved the work that was being asked of me. So, hit record or no hit record, I toured. My band and I would hop on a tour bus for months at a time, playing smoky bars, beautiful theaters, cornfields, restaurants, amphitheaters, schools—you name it, we played it. I wanted it so much, I was willing to work for it, and I made sure that everyone knew just how much being a country music singer meant to me.

Fame

Fame is a precarious thing. It wasn't the reason that I aspired to be an entertainer, but it happened whether I wanted it or not. For the most part, fame has never been a nuisance to me. In fact, when I have noticed my fame, I've liked it just fine. To me, it simply means that I'm having some measure of success with what I love the most. So, when I think of it that way, it's tolerable.

At times, however, being famous would encroach on that secret part of me. Like a low-hanging dark cloud steadily coming my way, sometimes fame is an ominous bearer of storm and anxiety. The more well known I became, the more people wanted to know about me. I understood, but I didn't like it, because those inquiries became less about my songs and career and more about my personal life.

I became a skilled liar. I learned early on in my life the pitfalls of lying. I didn't try it too often, but the couple of times I did, I got caught. My parents were experts in lie detection. They tripped me up by getting me to give them details. I'd tell the lie, then they'd somehow get me to expound upon it. They'd say, "Well, who all was there? What did you eat? Who cooked it? Who drove? What time did so-and-so's folks get home?" I'd give them all of my phony answers, but they wouldn't relent. They would ask another batch of questions, and I'd forget exactly what I'd already told them. Before I knew it, they'd find the inconsistencies in my story. Yeah, they were good. Then they'd explain to me that details are too hard to remember when you're lying. The truth will always catch up with you, they'd say.

So, when asked about my personal life during my career, I avoided details. I didn't make up stories about some bogus, nonexistent boyfriend who lived out of town. When people in the business asked about my holiday season, I didn't fill up my answer with what I thought would sound like a normal answer. I'd just say, "Oh, not much." The best thing about my brevity was that some people got used to my responses and just stopped asking. I think it caused me to be known by many as simply being an extremely private person. Even my managers at the time, Clarence, Bob, and Mark, didn't ask me questions, ever. Country music is like the military—don't ask, don't tell.

However, there were plenty of times with industry people, journalists, radio people, and fans that caused me to be sick to my stomach with fear. When asked personal questions that I simply didn't want to answer, I'd give my standard curt replies. "Oh, I'm not married, because I'm married to my work." "I'm just too busy to date." "That's kind of a personal question, don't you think?" I'd say playfully.

Inevitably, my avoiding the questions didn't always stop them from coming. When I realized that, I made the decision to make myself available to be questioned. I didn't hang out with many of my peers. I didn't go out for star-studded nights on the town and socialize with my coworkers. I didn't stay up late at night on the bus and engage in chitchat with the band and crew very often. Unfortunately, I think that approach caused me to gain a reputation for being cold and stuck-up. Other artists would say things to me like "You need to loosen up, have a little fun. Don't take it all so seriously."

Another thing that I did a little differently than other country music artists did was that I didn't party with radio folks. The radio community, by and large, decides who becomes a star and who does not. Sometimes artists are encouraged by their record labels to go hang out and have a good time with these radio program directors and radio consultants. And when I say "good time," this usually meant drinking with them. I never did it.

If you asked me how many radio guys have been inappropriate and disrespectful to me due to the fact that they've had about four too many drinks, the answer would have to be in the triple digits. When I was told by my label and by my managers that I needed to go hang out at some of these events, I did—I just did it differently. If the event was supposed to last from seven until midnight, I'd slip in at seven thirty and leave by eight thirty.

I really tried to look around and see how others whom I respected handled these situations. There is not a more professional or more revered person in our town than Reba McEntire. I was lucky to be around her quite a bit, as most of us were running in the same circles. She and I were also label mates on MCA Records at that time, which put me near her on even more occasions. Some celebrities on similar levels as Reba want the respect of others just because they are that famous, but they'll show up an hour late, throw tantrums, abuse their power, and then wonder why they aren't treated with higher regard. Not Reba McEntire. She shows up on time. She doesn't keep her fans waiting. She doesn't yell at her employees and belittle them. She starts her show on time and doesn't cut her show short by thirty minutes just because she's not "feeling it." Reba doesn't party or get drunk at the industry conventions that we all have to attend. Industry people and other artists alike show that woman an immense amount of respect because she's earned it— she deserves it. So when I'd see Reba and the way that she approached her work, I said to myself, "I'm going to try to emulate her." I have a strong suspicion that Reba took some notes on how to be a star from Dolly Parton. Dolly is the same way— a pro.

With some of my MCA label mates at a 2001 post–awards show party.
Left to right: Allison Moorer, Trisha Yearwood, George Strait,
Reba McEntire, me, and Gary Allan.

There has been an additional benefit for me in not hanging out and partying. When people have had three or four drinks and they start thinking that we're pals, they seem to lose sight of appropriate boundaries. When those walls of judgment start to fall, sometimes they feel just a little too comfortable with me and start to ask, "Why aren't you married?" I would do my best to change the subject, but took some comfort in knowing that they were so inebriated, they'd surely not remember a word of the conversation. I've been groped, grabbed, and made to listen to jokes that probably wouldn't have been told in my presence had alcohol not been involved, and those jokes and stories have been disgusting and at times frightening to me.

Imagine what it was like, being in the company of six relative strangers as they yucked it up, throwing drinks back and laughing at their own jokes about sex, oral sex, prison sex, gays, fags, dykes, lesbians, and the "N" word. You might wonder why I didn't just tell them off or leave the room in those particular instances. Many of those people held my future in their hands. I essentially had to grin and bear it. It was not unusual on a Monday morning to hear a true story of how a certain artist had pissed off a radio programmer and had his record dropped from their playlist. Granted, sometimes it was the fault of the artist for being an ass or arrogant or having made a drunken comment. Yes, there are just as many artists and label people who are jerks, and there are real consequences to be paid. So my way of doing it—not partaking of the party aspect of it—really spared me a lot of negative experiences. Having said that, I also want to say that not all radio folks are that way. There are many who are wonderful, smart, dedicated, happily married, happily single, respectful men and women who are talented at what they do, and I am pleased to call many of them my friends.

Knee-Deep in a River
and Dying of Thirst

Julia struggled with the fact that I was a public figure. She and I seldom went out together in Nashville, but when we did, it wasn't uncommon for someone to approach me to say hello. Sometimes it would be a fan, but usually it was someone in the music industry. When I was approached, I'd take just a couple of minutes to talk to them. I didn't mind it at all, but she did.

I recall being at a coffee shop near downtown Nashville with her when a song publisher came over to our table and started talking to me. She was sitting across from me, and the minute he got to the table she picked up her purse and told me that she'd be waiting in the car. I wrapped up my conversation with the publisher, then went out to the car, got in, and we had a pointed discussion about it.

"Why do you have to be so nice to them?" she asked. "Why can't you just let them say hello and then say hello back and leave it at that?"

It really bugged her that when someone would say hello, I'd ask them, "So how've you been? What's been going on?" Part of it was my being friendly and the other part was that I was probably genuinely curious about how they were doing.

It's not that Julia was unfriendly. Once she felt comfortable with someone, she was a talker, but she was shy around most folks. She scoffed at how the fans could love me so much without even knowing me at all.

Time and distance away from that relationship make me realize that maybe part of the reason she didn't want me to visit with people was because it was a reminder to her of who I am. She simply didn't want me to be known. She didn't want to see it, hear about it, or know about it. She despised my being a public figure because she could never be a part of it.

Julia was still in the music industry, and she worked closely with artists every day. She would come home and complain that most of them needed to take a class on how to be more professional, on how to work hard and do the things necessary to have a successful career. "Why can't they just do their job like you do yours? You're so dependable and you just do your work," she'd say. She, of all people, knew how hard an artist has to work. She said so herself. She knew exactly why I worked the way I did— because that's what it takes and nothing short of that will do. She just didn't want *me* to do it. Had I been in her position, I would've had resentment too. She was forced, out of necessity, to become invisible. This very issue started out as a tiny little splinter under the skin of our relationship, but as the months and years went by, it began to fester.

Brad

I met Brad Paisley in the spring of 1999. It was during a week-long industry event in Nashville called Country Radio Seminar. We were each making our rounds with radio stations, doing back-to-back interviews early one morning at the Union Station Hotel. All of the artists in country music make their way

Brad Paisley and I shared the stage every chance we got. 2000.
(Ron Newcomer)

to the different locations in Nashville where these stations are broadcasting via satellite to their listeners back home.

Brad was a new artist. In fact, I'd just become aware of him the night before. I had been watching country videos on TV, and they debuted a video from this new guy, Brad Paisley. I'd heard his first single, "Who Needs Pictures," and liked it, but when I saw the video from "He Didn't Have to Be" it blew me away. When I saw him the next morning, I told him that I loved his new record.

A week or so after that, I got a message from him. He told me that he and Tim Nichols, a writer in town, had started a song, and they wondered if I'd be interested in getting together with them to finish it. We met at my office at MCA Music and the three of us completed a song called "Not as in Love (as I'd Like to Be)."

I found Brad to be different than I'd anticipated. He was not some redneck cowboy with a simple mind. He was funny and had a certain wit that I enjoyed. We hit it off immediately, and I was pleased to find a new collaborator whom I could enjoy. Most professional songwriters will tell you that the days spent with other writers whom you don't really click with can be a form of torture.

During the next couple of months, Brad and I continued to share song ideas. There was one point at which I felt that he was getting the wrong idea about our friendship. His behavior and the things he'd say started to feel romantic in nature.

Julia and I were still trying to figure out how to make our individual lives and our relationship harmonious. Spending time with Brad was pleasant and would have been a much easier choice for me, but Julia was the one I loved.

I didn't want to lead Brad on, so I did what I've always had to do in situations like that—I pushed him away. I failed to return a couple of his calls, and finally he got the message. Another innocent person fell victim to my hiding. It was a cruel practice that I felt forced to use time and again.

The Slow Climb

In the summer of 1999, I was as busy as ever. "Single White Female" was slowly but steadily climbing the charts, and according to my manager and label we had a hit on our hands. The progress of a record is a day-to-day experience. It's like watching a long sporting event. Just as a football game takes

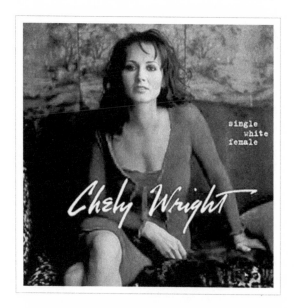

The cover of my fourth album, Single White Female, *released in 1999.*

strategy, luck, and a period of time to unfold, and there is no definite winner until the very end, a record climbing the charts is dramatic. I was on the road most of the time that summer, and the excitement was like nothing I'd ever known in my career. "Single White Female" was my tenth single to be released to radio, and the only hit I'd ever had was a Top 10 single called "Shut Up and Drive," from a previous album. We knew we had something bigger happening with "SWF."

The band and crew especially deserved this. I'm not kidding when I say I was happier for my band, my crew, my managers, and my support people than I was for myself. My drummer, Preston, had been with me since my first record and is still with me today. Many of these guys had hung in there with me, enduring endless tours, not much sleep, not a lot of money, only to see most of my singles not make it past #20 on the charts. So when it started to happen, it belonged to all of us and it felt great.

I remember the day that "SWF" went to #1 on the first of three charts. (At that time our industry acknowledged three charts—Gavin, Billboard, and R&R.) The Gavin chart was the first to announce "SWF" at the #1 position.

I was on the road. We were playing a big outdoor festival show with multiple acts. On days like that, we didn't really have much to do, as our sound checks typically took only thirty minutes. The band had done a morning sound check, and a few of us were on our way to a golf course to kill some time.

The golfing foursome that day was Preston, my keyboard player Jay (now in a band called Rascal Flatts), Joe Don (Rascal Flatts as well), and me. We had a great round of golf, a lot of laughs, and it was a gorgeous day. The runner van came to get us to take us back to the venue, and we were dropped off by the door of the tour bus behind the stage. As I stepped up onto the

With Rascal Flatts backstage in 2001. Jay (on my right) and Joe Don (on my left) met each other playing in my band. We share so many good memories.

bus, I took a quick peek out at the crowd and saw a sea of people having fun and enjoying the band that was onstage at the time. After the guys loaded the golf clubs into the storage bays below, they made their way to the front lounge of the forty-five-foot Prevost tour bus that we called home.

One of my managers, Mark, called for everyone to listen up. I knew that it wasn't going to be bad news, because he would've given that to me privately. Plus he was smiling. Then I thought he was going to tell us something about the show, perhaps that we'd be going on an hour late or something.

Mark said, "Lady and Gentlemen, I have an announcement to make. Today is a day to celebrate. I received a phone call from Clarence about two hours ago that our girl, Chely Wright, officially has the number one record in the nation today. 'Single White Female' is officially a number one record. We're number ONE!" Although I had a non-drinking policy on my bus, Mark had sprung for a bottle of Dom Pérignon and a dozen plastic champagne glasses. We toasted, sipped, hugged, high-fived, and laughed. I will never forget my hug with Preston, though, because it was a long, solid hug and we both cried. We had a great show, and it was a thrill for me to get to announce to the crowd of thirty thousand people that "Single White Female" had just gone to #1.

I went back to my hotel room that night to shower before getting on the bus to go to sleep. As usual, I called Julia on the phone to talk to her for a couple of minutes before she got into bed. We talked for a little bit, and then I told her that "Single White Female" had made it to #1. I said it casually because I knew what her reaction would be, and I didn't want to set myself up for disappointment. I'd learned a long time before not to expect her to show any excitement over my successes. Her response was, as I anticipated, "Oh, I didn't know it was still climbing." It was as if I'd told her that it had rained that day. Why couldn't she just be happy for me? I wanted her to have all that she wanted out of her career—why couldn't she just want the same for me?

She knew I was an artist when she met me. It's not like she thought she was getting involved with a schoolteacher who suddenly decided to try to become a famous country music singer. She knew who I was and what my ambitions were. Every mark of success that I enjoyed pulled us further and further apart. The hiding, the compartmentalizing, the non-acknowledgment of my partner were surely killing us.

Radio, magazines, and newspapers—they all wanted a few minutes of my time, and I was more than pleased to oblige. My cell phone rang off the hook the day we went #1 on the Billboard chart.

I had just arrived back in Nashville that morning from a show in the Northeast. The bus rolled into town about 7 a.m., and I got out of my bunk about 7:30. I gathered my things, as we had a couple of days off and I needed to do my laundry. I piled my stuff into my car, which was sitting in the Kroger parking lot just outside of downtown Nashville. I was in my pajama bottoms, a T-shirt, and slippers, standing in front of the dairy products in Kroger when my cell phone rang. It was my record label calling. The MCA radio promotion team was yelling and whistling, calling to tell me that we had just gone to #1 on the Billboard chart. This was a big deal. I squealed with delight and told them that I was in the grocery store and that I'd call them back the minute I got to my house.

I grabbed my creamer and headed to the check-out aisle. The store had virtually no customers in it. As I approached the front of the store, I cut through the potato chip aisle. There was a young man, maybe twenty-one years old, stocking the supply of chips. He had on a work shirt that said FRITO-LAY on it. He had tattoos up and down both forearms and piercings in his nose, ears, lip, and eyebrow. I stopped right next to him. He looked up and made eye contact with me, and I said, "I'm number one." To which he replied, "Huh?" I said, "My record just went to number one on the Billboard chart!" He paused, then said, "Cool." Before he knew it, I had thrown my arms around his shoulders, still clutching a cell phone in one hand and Coffee-mate Fat Free Hazelnut Creamer in the other, and hugged him.

My phone started to ring a couple of hours later and just didn't stop. Voice mail after voice mail, conversation after conversation filled with words of congratulations. I heard from the heads of other record labels, other artists' managers, publishers, producers with whom I'd previously worked, songwriters, publicists, musicians, and radio people. I will never forget those calls.

The best, however, were from other artists. They were the most important to me because I knew that they, and only they, knew exactly what it felt like to have something you've dreamed about your whole life come true. I heard from Reba McEntire, Vince Gill, Brett Favre, Faith Hill, Kenny Chesney, Martina McBride, Loretta Lynn, Trisha Yearwood, Kix Brooks, and

Garth Brooks, and I even got a basket of flowers delivered to my house from Alan and Denise Jackson. It was truly one of the most memorable days of my life.

And to top it all off, my best friend, Chuck, was flying into Nashville that day for a visit that we'd planned several weeks earlier. We decided to do something crazy—well, crazy for me. We rented a limo and rode around Nashville dialing up my band and crew. We had an impromptu gathering at a Mexican restaurant just off Music Row. The Iguana had a big outdoor deck and was an ideal spot for twenty of us to eat and drink until our bellies and our hearts were ready to explode. It was the perfect night— except for the fact that Julia wasn't there. I'd invited her, but she didn't come.

About a month later, MCA Records and the publishers of "Single White Female" arranged an official #1 party. These parties to celebrate #1 records are commonly scheduled during office hours on Music Row to ensure that everyone involved in the record's success is able to attend. The artist and writers get to invite anyone they want, and it's not unusual for family members and close friends to fly in from out of state to be there for this special event.

I invited everyone. The night before the party, Chuck, Julia, another friend, and I were at my house in Kingston Springs, just outside of Nashville. Chuck asked Julia where she thought we should meet on Music Row the next day before the party so we could go over together. That's when she told him that she wasn't sure if she was going. It was the first I'd heard of it—I had just assumed that she'd be there.

I asked her why and she said, "Why do I need to be there? You've got all of those people who just love you so much and kiss your ass and tell you that you're the greatest—what difference does it make if I'm there?"

Later that night, when she and I got into bed, I asked her to please reconsider because it would mean the world to me if she

Some of the best friends I've had in my life. Left to right: Preston, Jeff, Jan,
me, Anne Marie, Judy, and Chuck after my show for Fleet Week
on the U.S.S. Intrepid, *New York City. 2005.*

went. She said, "Let me see how my day goes." I went to sleep
feeling pretty good about her showing up after all. The next day
I looked for her at the party. She did not attend—she went to a
yoga class instead.

Although I was hurt, I knew Julia was hurt as well. I began to
feel that our fragile secret relationship could not survive my
career, her loathing of it, and the speculation about my personal
life that came with it.

Because I had so many people who supported and loved me,
she'd often ask me why I needed that from her. For years, I tried
to explain to her that I could have a million people screaming my
name and cheering for me, but that didn't fill the spot in my
heart that one "Congratulations, I'm excited for you, and I'm
proud of you" from her would fill. I was standing knee-deep in a
river and dying of thirst.

All the Way to Memphis

As much as I fantasized about living in the same house with Julia and sharing a life like normal people did, the thought of actually doing that, as a gay couple, scared me to death. In many ways, I liked our situation and had learned how to make it fit into my life. When Julia and Phillip decided to divorce, I knew that everything was about to change and that the change between "them" would certainly affect "us."

Phillip moved out of their home, and Julia did something that I never expected. She pulled away from me and started dating a man. He was a new artist on Music Row who was trying to secure a record contract. She didn't tell me that she was dating him at first, but I heard through the small grapevine of Music Row. People would mention their relationship to me, unaware that they were actually informing me that my girlfriend had a new boyfriend.

It was 1999. I was having hit records and touring like crazy, but finally I had a rare, much-needed night off at home. I wanted to see her, to talk to her. I needed to hear it from her that she was seeing this man. I had been with a friend earlier in the day and Julia's name had come up. He mentioned that he knew she had plans that night to attend a Nashville Predators hockey game with Tommy Mason and that the two were an "item" now.

While driving home, I called her cell phone and left a message asking her to call me when she got a chance. She didn't call back. Around ten o'clock that night, I put my little dog, Miss Minnie, in the car and drove to her house. Her car was in the driveway. I knocked on the door and as she opened it, I could see that she was still in her work clothes, that she'd just gotten home. I asked her if I could come in so we could talk, but she said that she was just so tired and wanted to go to bed.

I asked her point-blank if she was dating Tommy Mason and she said that she was. I started to cry and didn't make any attempt to hide it from her. Between the tears and trying to look at her through a screen door, I couldn't see her clearly. My head felt as fuzzy as my vision, but I was able to make a declaration without any hesitation. I told her that I was willing to do whatever it took to be with her. I told her that I didn't care about anything but being happy and that she was the one thing I just didn't want to go without. She didn't even take five seconds to ponder what I had just said to her. She was so cold and dismissive when she said, "No, Chely. It's just too hard. We can't do this anymore. I can't do it anymore. It's never gonna work. You and I are never gonna work."

She closed the door and turned off the porch light while I was standing there, on that same porch where I had been welcomed for so many years. Now it was dark and colder than it had ever been. I got on I-40 to drive to my house, one exit away, but I didn't take the exit. Instead, I drove all the way to Memphis and back, with Minnie asleep the whole time in my lap.

Bites and Stings

As I made my way home from that impromptu trip to Memphis, I had a new understanding of being all alone. I had painted myself so masterfully into a corner, and I didn't have a friend or a family member to turn to. When my friends would suffer a broken heart, their mothers would be the first to nurture them, saying, "Everything's going to be okay, honey. I love you, and I'll help you through this." It was times like those that I felt cheated that I didn't have a mother in my life. My mother hadn't died. She was alive and relatively well back in Kansas.

My parents had been divorced for more than three years, and I'd barely seen or spoken to my mother in that time period. In fact, things got really weird upon my return from that tour I'd taken to Japan a few years before, the one that began with the bon voyage phone call from Aunt Char—"Have a great trip, your family's falling apart."

When I got back to the States from the shows in Japan, I didn't go home to Nashville because I had domestic tour dates for the remainder of the year. I got a message on my answering machine from my dad giving me a different phone number to reach him. I called him at his new, run-down apartment, and he said that Jeny had visited him to help put some touches on the place that would make it feel a little more like a home. It hurt to hear my dad's voice shake as he told me that my mom said their marriage was really over. He told me that he was going to get her back, but I didn't have high hopes that he would succeed. I was excited for both of my parents to get a brand-new start. My biggest fear for my father was that he might start drinking again.

"Dad, whatever you do, don't drink, okay? It won't help."

"I won't, Chel. I promise."

I was curious about how my mother was doing, so I called and left her a message. *A* message. Just one. Maybe I should've left a dozen so she'd know that I really cared, but I didn't.

My mom and I had stayed in close contact during my first couple of years in Nashville, and I'd share with her the details about my job at Country Music USA and my plans on how I was going to try to get a recording contract. My dad would occasionally get on the phone, but he'd usually be in the background on her end of the line, interjecting and asking his own questions. Even though I continued to have regular communication with her, it became increasingly difficult for me to deal with her.

My mom was never easy to get along with, but when I was a young child, then an adolescent, and later a teenager living under "her roof," we all deferred to her, including my father. I thought the way we were was normal. It took me well into my adulthood and experiencing being around my friends and seeing them with their parents to understand that my family dynamic was a recipe for years of pain—for all involved.

One of the first times I recall standing up for myself was just after I'd turned twenty years old. I was living in Nashville and had wrapped up my second season at Opryland, so I bought myself a plane ticket home to spend a week with my mom and dad.

The three of us were driving home from having dinner in a nearby town. The radio was playing a song by a new country singer whom I liked a lot. I said, "Oooh, turn that up. I love her voice." My dad cranked it a notch as we cruised down the two-lane road with our bellies full of chicken-fried steak and apple crisp. Within seconds, my mom reached over and snapped the radio dial to the off position.

"Hey!" I exclaimed, "I was listening to that."

"She can't sing," my mother said.

I felt like a little kid in that backseat of my parents' car and was inclined to let her, as usual, rule the moment. I stewed for a bit; then my mouth opened up, and twenty years of frustration came out. In the most empowered, placid delivery of my life—to that point—I said, "That's your opinion, Mom. Maybe you don't like her voice, or maybe you don't think this is a good song, but she *can* sing. She's a professional country music singer, and I'm sure she makes millions of dollars singing that song. I heard her sing live on the Grand Ole Opry a couple of weeks ago, and she was one of the best singers there. So although *you* may not think she can sing, a whole lot of other people do. Including me."

"You don't know what you're talking about," she said in a low, monotone reply.

I could see the top third of my dad's face in the rearview mirror, and after he'd dedicated his stare straight ahead to the asphalt and the dotted lines, he cut his glare up and over, and that stare reflected, then connected with mine. I saw the familiar *"I wish you hadn't gone and done that"* in his eyes, and that look ricocheted a hundred times off metal, plastic, fabric, and glass on the inside of that car.

Something was different inside of me though. I knew I wasn't deserving of the title about to be assigned to me: The One Who Ruined a Nice Night Out. My dad didn't say a word, my mom was silent, and for the first time in my life, I didn't try to fix it. I don't know how I knew, but I did, with full certainty, that it wasn't mine to fix.

The gravel crunched under the tires as we pulled into the driveway. My mother made a point of being the first out of the car (not an easy thing for her to do, considering polio had crippled her right leg), but in order to be the first to slam your door shut, you have to be the first one out. When we got inside, my mother went straight to my parents' bedroom and locked the door behind her. My dad sat in his La-Z-Boy recliner that I'd bought for him the year before, the one he spent so much time in after we brought him home from the hospital to recover from his emergency triple-bypass surgery.

With my mother locked in her bedroom and my father making his anger known only to the remote control, I went to the guest bedroom and put on my pajamas. I sat on the edge of the bed and honestly did consider knocking on her door, telling her that I wasn't sure what had gotten into me and that I was sorry. No. I wouldn't do it, I thought. I didn't know exactly what *to* do because this territory was new to me, but I knew what I wouldn't do. I would not shrink this time.

I stayed in the guest room and was reading a book when I heard my dad's voice through his famous clenched teeth saying to my mother, "Cheri, open up this door." She opened the door, and I could hear both of their voices rising in pitch and volume at the exact same moments—ensuring that neither heard what the other was saying. This was a skill they'd refined over the years. My dad exited their bedroom, slamming the door for effect and went back to his chair. It was late, nearly midnight. I went to the living room to talk to him.

"She won't come out. I don't know what's wrong with her, Chel. It's getting worse. Since you kids left, she's just mean as a snake, even more than before. I don't know what to do," my dad said with the look of a man who'd been pushing a fifty-car freight train up a hill.

I felt confident and healthy when I said, "I don't know what you should do either, Dad, but I know what I'm gonna do."

While my mom and dad had been in their bedroom arguing, I had been on the telephone changing my departure out of Kansas City from four days later to the next morning. When I told my dad that I was scheduled to fly out sooner than later and that I needed a ride to the airport, I thought he was going to cry, but he didn't.

His tense shoulders slumped in defeat when he said, "Please don't go. Can't you stay for me? Your visit home is all I've been looking forward to. Please don't let her ruin it. Let me go talk to her again."

He came into the guest room a while later, and I was packing my things.

"I told her you were going home," he said.

I knew before he went in there that she wasn't going to be moved by the news.

"What time do you have to be there in the morning"? he asked.

Together, we figured out the travel time to KCI Airport, which was nearly two hours away, and then we said good night.

I got up early and loaded my things into the trunk of the car. I went back inside the house to use the restroom, and although I knew that my mother wouldn't approach me to say good-bye, I thought she might make herself visible in the kitchen or something to give me one last chance to tell her how sorry I was. She didn't.

My dad and I talked the entire ride up to the city. The only thing I remember specifically saying to him is, "Dad, I'm not married to her. I don't have to stay. I'm just her daughter."

It would be more than a month before I would speak to my mother again. She simply had no intention of calling me, so I broke down. I called her and apologized. I felt happy to have fixed it and to have reopened the lines of communication with her, but I knew I shouldn't have had to be the one to go groveling and begging her for forgiveness.

Five years later, when I left that message on her answering machine, checking in on her to find out how she was doing, in light of my hearing through the grapevine that she and my dad were divorcing, I felt something familiar. Making the phone call stung. Here I was, again, initiating a phone call that I shouldn't necessarily have had to put into motion. Isn't it standard protocol that when the parents decide to get divorced, they call the kids and tenderly break the news to them and say things like, "This isn't going to change a thing, honey. I love you and your dad still loves you. We'll always be a family in one way or another"? Or "Kids, we still care about each other; we just aren't in love anymore. Our splitting up should actually make things a little less difficult for all of us"? Isn't that how it goes?

I finally heard from my mother a couple of weeks after I returned from Japan. I was in a hotel room in Kansas City, and I was scheduled to play a show at an outdoor theater located on the property of an amusement park called Worlds of Fun that night. I was arranging my hair and makeup products and my wardrobe items in preparation, when the phone rang. Expecting it to be my tour manager or one of my band guys calling from another room, I answered in a silly voice, "Heeellllllooooo."

"Ms. Wright?" inquired the person on the other end.

I gave an embarrassed cough and replied, in normal fashion, "This is she."

"I have someone here in the lobby who would like to speak to you. I'll put her on." It was the front desk at the hotel.

"Hey, Chel, it's your mother. What room are you in? I'll come up."

Hearing that my mother was on her way up was not bad news to me. In fact, I was sort of excited. My mom had come to see me, and doesn't that always feel good to a kid? Within seconds, she knocked on the door. As I pulled it open toward me, I said a protracted, "Heeeey."

Standing next to my mother was a man I'd never seen. I said, "Uuuhhh, hi. Come in." I'm sure I looked confused, because I was. I went quickly through the index of my mind as to who this fella might be. My parents knew a lot of people from their worlds of construction, music, coon hunting, and card playing, but I was coming up blank trying to figure out who this guy (not much older than my brother) was.

As they walked in, my mom said, "This is Larry."

"Hey, Larry, nice to meet you," I said and shook his hand. "Come on in and sit down, you guys. Let me go ahead and get my curling iron heated up." I stepped into the bathroom, plugged it in, and walked back into the other room. They had chosen to sit on the bed, so I sat in one of the two chairs flanking a small table by the window that gave an expansive view of the Missouri River. We made small talk for a couple of minutes, and then what she was saying started to sound muffled. I must have fallen behind on my half of the conversation (half, not a third—Larry never said a word) because what I was seeing was actually starting to seep in.

My mother and this man, whom I knew nothing about, were sitting next to each other. This man had his left arm behind her and she was leaning into that arm.

I was trying to join the discussion about the Kansas City Chiefs' last game, but the top of my throat started to contract, and I began to cry. Still, I tried to remain engaged.

"Why are you crying?" my mother demanded.

She turned to him and had a five-second, nonlinguistic *I told you this was going to happen* conversation. "Let's go," she said.

She left and he followed behind.

My mother called me a few days later to tell me that I had made an ass out of myself and that I embarrassed her in front of her friend.

A few months later Larry became my stepfather.

After that, she was busy, and I was hopeful that if she could find happiness maybe she wouldn't be so difficult for everyone else to deal with. But it didn't turn out that way. The new version of my mother became even more polarizing, especially to her three kids. She often went away for months, even years, at a time. When she and I did speak on the phone, the conversations were bizarre—it was as if she were a stranger. She'd tell stories about our family's past, which I recalled but she changed the details. Jeny, Chris, and I would call one another on the phone and marvel at the staggering contrasts between our collective memory and hers. No matter what my mother and I were talking about, she would always ask me if I had spoken to my father. I would answer honestly. When I said, "Yes, I've talked to him," the phone would go dead.

She wanted me to expel my father from my life, and she wanted me to hate him. She'd tell me reasons and stories of why I should do both, most of which I didn't believe. The stories I might believe or actually know to be true weren't any of my business. If she could not govern, she was unable to be involved. I consistently tried to work things out. I'd write a long letter or make that phone call. After I'd eat enough crow, my mom, with an imperious pride and sense of having won some battle, would usually let me back in. Until I made her angry again. Which never took long.

Her unwillingness or inability to be a part of my life corresponded with my hiding my homosexuality from her, which was convenient for me. On the other hand, my mother's absence fell smack dab in the years when I probably needed her the most. I suppose I still had a fantasy of a selfless, kind-hearted mother.

"You and Julia will work this out. You two love each other so much, and you're so good together. I know you're in a tough spot having to keep your relationship a secret, but your secret is safe with me. I just want you to be happy, hon. You go do your shows, and when you get back to Nashville, I'll be at your house and I'll stay for a couple of weeks. Everything's going to be okay. Love wins out in the end, Squirrelly, and nothin's more important than your happiness."

Love Is Love

The day after Julia closed the door on me, and on our relationship, I climbed aboard the tour bus with a fake smile and a bleeding heart. At that time, my record was one of the most popular in the country, and the crowds at my concerts were large and excited to see me. I couldn't be distraught in front of my band and crew over a broken relationship—a relationship that they had never known to exist. I gave up. On that trip, I did my best to let go of Julia.

We ended that tour just a week or so before Christmas of 1999. I was scheduled for eight days off, with my next show slated to be the New Year's Eve celebration in Salt Lake City to ring in the year 2000. I was looking forward to my holiday with my family. We were getting together at my brother's house in Yuma, Arizona.

I was an expert at telling my family about my life without actually telling them anything. No one knew my secret. Sometimes there is something so demoralizing about being the gay relative (in the closet or out of the closet) who travels to family functions. Because we often show up as a single person, without a mate, we are relegated to be the one to sleep on the floor or on the sofa or even with a niece or nephew in a twin Spider-Man or Strawberry Shortcake bed. I don't know what that's about, but it's as if, since I never came home for the holidays with a husband

and baby in tow, I was viewed as not yet being a grown-up. I did want to be there with my family, but more than anything I wanted to be able to let my false front crumble to the ground. It seemed that there was nowhere for me to be me.

For months, I'd called home to my answering machine in Nashville from all over the world, hoping to get a message from Julia. That call never came, and I had stopped calling twenty times a day to check the machine.

In Yuma, we drank pots of coffee and took our time preparing a meal that would be served at around three o'clock.

After I'd set the table with all of the best dishes, napkins, and candles that we had, I called my answering machine to pick up messages from friends and family who would have checked in on Christmas Day. Six messages in was a message from Julia.

She told me that she missed me and that being away from me was killing her and to please call her back. I went outside and called her on my cell phone.

She was prepared to do anything and everything to be together. She asked me if I'd consider taking her back and trying to make it work. My answer was yes.

I returned to Nashville and we spent what days I had left of my holiday together. We talked, we cried, we apologized, we forgave, and we started making plans to live our lives together. A few days after I returned from my Salt Lake City show, I put a down payment on our brand-new home, which would be built in West Nashville. It would take six months to build.

In My Own Home

The duality of my life became more pronounced, and I became even more expert in the betrayal of myself as an artist and as a woman. Work dinners, awards shows, receptions—I went alone. I would go do my appearance, satisfy my obligations, then go home to her. Once I did get home, there was never a question as to how my night had been. She did not want to hear a thing about it. It was hard for her to see me do all of that and for her not to be acknowledged as my partner. I wanted her to be happy for my successes, but because she was so excluded she hated my success. I had been conditioned over the years not to discuss my career with her.

If I had a new photo shoot to study and review for an upcoming album, I had to be careful. While she was gone to her job on Music Row, I'd spread the photos out on the dining room table and make my notes as to which ones were my picks for the album cover, for the publicity department, and so on and so forth. She came home every night at about six o'clock, so I knew that by five forty-five I needed to have it all put away and out of sight. If I had had a good week with radio airplay or a bad week, I said nothing. I wish I'd had the courage at that time to come out of the closet and that I'd had enough love for myself not to allow my partner to deny me her full support in all areas of my life.

*I had a private life and a very public life. Part of being a
public person is attending special events and award shows.
This photo of me with Lance Bass was taken backstage at the
Country Music Association Awards in Nashville in 2000.
'N Sync performed on the show that night too.*

Julia wasn't out either and didn't want to be. Her mother lived down the street from us, and they enjoyed a very close relationship. She is an eighty-five-year-old, old-fashioned Catholic who attended Mass every single day. I was close to her mother as well. I was, as her mother called me, her surrogate daughter. I spoke to her doctors, got her prescriptions at times, did chores for her at her house, took her car-shopping for her green Volkswagen Bug that she'd wanted so badly, took her on our vacations with us—she was family to me. Julia had never told her that we were together, although I don't know how she didn't figure it out.

I wasn't pushing my partner to come out, but she pushed me. Rather than my coming out completely, she wanted me to confide my situation to some of my circle of friends. She said that it would make her feel more acknowledged. I have to tell you that for all intents and purposes, they knew—I just wasn't about to confirm it for them. My friends and employees treated her with respect and tried to include her in everything, but she pushed it all away. I'd explain to her that there was no need for me to confirm with them that I was gay and that she was my partner. My biggest concern in doing that was that the minute I told them, I was putting them in a position to have to lie for me. My friends were continually questioned: "Is Chely gay?" As long as I didn't confirm it with them, they could honestly say, "If she is, she's never told me." It was, to my way of thinking, best to keep it that way.

Our reclusive ways were fine with us in most other ways because we simply enjoyed each other so much. We had a beautiful home, gorgeous gardens, adorable pets (dogs and fish), hiking, biking, vacations, holidays, cooking, cleaning, movies, Scrabble, jokes, talking—we never ran out of things to talk about. We had a life. We had a good life. Everyone struggles in intimate relationships, but I believe that the hiding and the secret of our being gay caused irreparable damage.

Rumors

Every day is a battle when you hide. On a regular basis, the tabloids and other useless media try to reveal that certain people are gay. When this happens to a public person—when the speculation makes it to print—I get sick to my stomach. I just imagine what the targeted celebrity is going through. In small ways, I know what he or she is experiencing. Although I have never been publicly written about in the tabloids regarding my sexuality, it's been a rumor about me for years in Nashville. I'm not sure how it started, but it did. Let me be clear: I am and always have been gay, but the rumor that circulated so wildly early on in my career had not even one grain of truth to it. Really ironic, I suppose.

The first I ever heard of it was in 1994. I was a songwriter at PolyGram on Music Row, and one of my publishers, Daniel Hill, called me on the phone. He and I were casually dating at the time, but I was in love with Julia, so dating Daniel was a desperate attempt to distract myself. He called me and said, "I have to tell you something." I said, "Okay." He proceeded to tell me a story that was circulating about me.

The story was that a bus driver of mine had allegedly walked in on me having sex with a woman in the back lounge of my bus. I have heard that that fiction has been out there, and it has been told and retold for nearly fifteen years now. I think I know which disgruntled ex-employee of mine made it up.

Let me address this stupid rumor that my employee caught me having sex in the back of the bus. It never happened. I have had sex only once in the back of my tour bus, and it was with Brad Paisley. As exciting and scandalous as that old tale was, it never happened.

I have been aware during my career, when I meet other artists or am around other artists, that they've heard that rumor— among others, I'm sure. I know that when I leave the room, more than likely they discuss the topic. Daniel told me of the story that he'd heard and asked me, "Did that happen?" To which I replied, "No, that did not happen." We left it at that.

"Hard to Be a Husband,
Hard to Be a Wife"

In the fall of 2000, it was time to start deciding on songs for *Never Love You Enough,* my follow-up album to *Single White Female,* and that meant digging through thousands of songs penned by Nashville's very capable tunesmiths and ones I'd come up with too. I really did like the song Brad Paisley, Tim Nichols, and I had written the previous year, so I recorded it for my new album.

I was working at The Tracking Room on Music Row, trying my best to make an album that would continue the career momentum I was enjoying at that time. I loved how the initial tracks were sounding, so in between sessions, I called Brad and asked him if he wanted to come over and hear what my producers and I had done with our song.

He showed up a little while later. The other musicians were at lunch, and it was just the two of us at the mixing console. We listened and both agreed that it was going to be a good recording of a good song. There was an awkward pause, and then he said, "Can I ask you something?" I said, "Sure." He said, "Why didn't you return my calls?" I knew exactly what he was talking about, but I skirted the issue. I reassured him that there was no real reason why I didn't, that I must've just gotten busy and forgot. The excuse felt foreign as it came out of my mouth because it isn't "me" to forget to call people back. I may get busy, but I'm aware at all times to whom I owe a response by phone and by e-mail. I don't forget things like that, but I was hoping that he'd accept my excuse. He did and we easily became friends again.

Julia and I were struggling more than usual during that time. My star was still on the rise, and I was having the kind of success that I'd always dreamed of. She was also climbing the corporate ladder at her job. I was thrilled and supportive of her and resented the fact that she wasn't for me.

I was also feeling smothered by increasing questions from my industry, the press, and the fans about my personal life. Again, that's part of fame. Not only do people want to hear your music, they want to know your story. I got nervous and I started to real-ize that Julia and I weren't doing that well and that we'd proba-bly not survive the storm of speculation and inquiry. I began having thoughts about wanting to be normal and actually just making a choice to live a straight life. If I wasn't going to be able to have Julia as my partner and if we weren't going to make it . . . well, I decided that if I was going to be unhappy and unful-filled anyway, why not just try to be with a man.

I felt resentful toward her, and I had grown tired of down-playing, in my own home, a large part of myself. I had dreamed of being a successful country artist since I was four years old, and it had come true. I was hurt by her demands, overt and subtle, that my career be left outside the door when I came home to her. I was trying hard to hold on to her, but I was also doing things that would push her away, things that I knew would break us. And that's why I allowed my relationship with Brad to grow. Self-destructive behavior is common among closeted gays, and I'm sure there are professionals who can tell you the clinical rea-sons why we do this to ourselves, but I can't. In my case, I did it because I felt discomfort about where I was in my life, and although I didn't quite know what to do to remedy my situation, I made a decision to just do something—anything.

So I did. Brad and I began to be involved on a different level, romantically. We had a lot in common. We were both very dedicated to our careers, we were both in love with the tradition of country music, we shared a respect for the Grand Ole Opry, and we shared a sense of responsibility to be good role models. Neither of us had ever done a drug in our lives, and aside from his occasional cigar, neither of us had even tried smoking. I loved that Brad didn't drink alcohol. I seldom drank, but if I'd have a glass of wine with a nice meal he didn't make a judgment on it that I could tell. He had a strong faith, and although I didn't agree with some of his religious beliefs and he didn't agree with some of mine, we had a mutual respect. I thought he had a good way of managing his life and his career, and I felt that if I was going to compromise and be with a man, he'd be an amazing choice. We laughed a lot and he had quickly become one of my best friends.

Brad and I spent a lot of time together in Nashville, and we

With Brad Paisley in 2000.

were touring together too. Our days on the road were easily integrated because we had similar habits and similar relationships with our band guys and crew members. We were each laid-back and didn't require extra attention or babysitting by our tour managers. If I needed something and my tour manager wasn't around, Brad's tour manager would help me out and vice versa. We'd ride on each other's buses, our drivers started to become pals, and our band guys were hanging out too. In the beginning, because I'd had a little more success than Brad, he was opening the shows. We started to come onstage during each other's performances and sing together here and there. Then he started to gain more and more success, and it quickly became a co-headlining bill. Of course, there were also shows that started to sprinkle in there where he was the headliner and I was his opening act. We'd laugh about how suddenly things can change in show business. I was thrilled for him and he was equally happy for me. We didn't compete; we considered ourselves a team. We wrote and produced songs together for my record and for his. I think we both had an understanding of each other's sacrifice and talent, and it was a nice change for me, to have a partner who cheered me on. I had just been nominated by the Academy of Country Music for Female Vocalist of the Year, and he had a nomination for New Male Vocalist of the Year. There was a notable ease to the whole thing.

One night while we were writing a song, we started talking about people's speculation about whether or not we were together as a couple. I did not want to publicly acknowledge our relationship, period. He did, and of course he didn't understand why I had such an aversion to it. I didn't want to because I'd made it my policy to never talk about my private life. If I started talking about my relationship with him, I feared that it would set a new precedent for me to openly discuss things like that. There was so much that I was hiding, I didn't want anyone to feel that my private life was no longer "off limits."

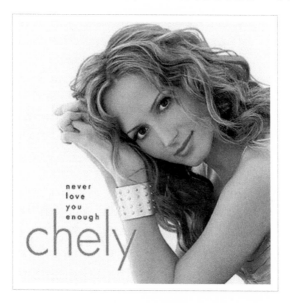

The cover of my fifth studio album, Never Love You Enough. *The year 2001 was a critical time in my career. There was a lot of expectation that this album would go beyond the success of* Single White Female.

I also knew that Julia didn't know what was really going on between Brad and me. I think there was a part of me that wanted her to know. I was on self-destruct. He loved the attention we were getting as a suspected couple, and he told me that he was having trouble not shouting it from the rooftops that he was in love with me. Oh, no. Love. He confessed his love to me. There were so many ways in which I did love him, but I was not in love with him. The first song we wrote together, as I mentioned before, was "Not as in Love (as I'd Like to Be)."

Brad continued to tell me that our being officially a couple would be good for our careers, and I knew he was right. We both had hit records, and the fans liked the thought of us together, in love. I was tortured by my reality. We were sharing an intimate relationship, and that was difficult for me in so many ways. I was still in love with Julia. I prayed to fall out of love with her.

Being physical with Brad did not come quickly or easily for me. After all, I am gay. I often cried during those moments of physical intimacy, and I have no idea what he made of it when I cried. Another reason why I didn't want to confirm my relationship with Brad was because I knew that it would eventually end, and somewhere in the back of my mind I wondered about the probability of my being outed. It was a real concern for me. The last thing I wanted to happen was for Brad to publicly declare his love for me, only to have the world find out someday that I am gay. I couldn't stand the thought of the humiliation that could cause Brad.

My being with Brad did squelch some of the speculation that people had about me. I began to think that if Julia and I didn't make it and Brad and I did . . . it just might be possible I'd escape this whole "gay thing" entirely. I began to hope it would play out that way and that any old rumors that I might be gay would be proven wrong. I just knew I'd be the one to take the hit, so to speak. I knew my heart would have to be willing to settle. I tried, I swear I did.

Brad didn't try to keep our relationship a secret with his friends and family. Why would he? Everyone in his world that was close to him knew about it. That was okay with me, as I came to adore most of his friends and the people around him. He liked my friends too, I think. A few of my good male friends are gay, and Brad knew that if he was going to be in my life, he was going to be around people "like that." We'd discussed the gay issue before and Brad's position on it was religiously based. He was a strict Christian and adhered to the belief that the Bible clearly says homosexuality is a sin. He expressed to me on many occasions that being gay is more than likely a result of someone's having been molested or that it is a choice. He is not alone in his thinking—especially in Nashville, in the South, and in the culture of country music. I made my case to him that I thought he was wrong and that most gays I know swear that it is not a choice. Nevertheless, once he did spend time with the gay men in my life, he liked them a lot. One time he said to me when discussing one of those friends, "Hey, I like the guy, even though he's gay. I sat at the dinner table with him, anyway, didn't I?"

Brad and I wrote a song that we thought was telling of who we were. The premise of it was that each of us, especially lately, had been asked so many questions about why each of us was unmarried or not engaged. I guess he started giving the response to people that I'd been giving my entire career: "I'm too busy, too focused on my career, and I'm married to my music." So we wrote a song that we sang together called "Hard to Be a Husband, Hard to Be a Wife."

We began to perform it at our shows and on the *Grand Ole*

From the CBS "Grand Ole Opry 75th Anniversary Celebration." Brad and I sang our song, "Hard to Be a Husband, Hard to Be a Wife." Garth Brooks (on my right) was also on the show. 2000.

Opry when the occasion would arise. Then we were invited by the Grand Ole Opry and the CBS television network to perform our song on a primetime network television special. It was a TV special that marked the 75th anniversary of the Grand Ole Opry, and we were the only non-members of the Opry who were asked to be a part of the show. It was the night of my thirtieth birthday and a highlight of my career—an amazing moment for both of us. The song was recorded live from the show and shortly after that, it began to be played on the radio. We'd be doing a show somewhere and people would yell out to us or hold up a sign that asked us to sing it, and we always did. We ended up getting a CMA (Country Music Association) nomination for Vocal Event of the Year for that song and record.

Brad is a thinker, a planner, and nothing that happens in his life just happens. He knows what he wants, forms a plan accordingly, and executes the plan. This is not a pejorative observation of him at all. In fact, I liked that about him. Anything he sets his mind to, he accomplishes. This was another quality that I admired and had put in the pros column of my figurative pros-and-cons list for Brad Paisley. I liked a person with vision, with the work ethic to follow through, and with the confidence to go after what he wanted. The problem was that he was now telling me that he wanted me . . . forever. He was starting to talk to me about forever and how someday he was going to want to marry me. Okay, now his characteristics of vision, focus, and resolve were landing solidly in the cons column of my list. I was scared.

I asked him if we could slow down. This came out of the blue to him because we really didn't seem to have any problems. Well, except for the tiny little fact of my being a lesbian. I was hoping that I'd just fall out of favor with him. No such luck.

There was a night on the road, just outside of L.A., that was particularly dramatic. I was doing my best to pull away from him. I wasn't very good at it, because it was all based on things that were false. For example, during the day of that show I talked to him in my dressing room about how I needed space. He didn't understand any of my reasons, and rightfully so—they didn't make sense. He left my dressing room, frustrated, I'm sure, but respecting my request to be left alone for the day. Then I ruined it. There was something that happened backstage that was funny or weird. I don't remember the details. But I just had to tell him, and I knocked on his dressing room door, grinning from ear to ear, to tell him this hilarious story that I just knew he'd want to hear, because we loved that kind of thing. The problem with all of that was that I forgot that I was supposed to be pulling away from him. It slipped my mind that I was "going through something and needed space" from him. Just as I imagined, he laughed at the story I'd come to tell him. Then his argument was, "Come on, Chel—don't we have fun? Don't we just 'fit'?" I didn't have a good argument why we didn't. I said I didn't want to talk about it.

I asked my tour manager, Joe Morris, to get me a ride back to the hotel near LAX. We were scheduled to fly out early the next morning to Phoenix for another show with Brad, and I just wanted to get to my room and get some sleep. I was back in my room and Brad started to call my cell phone. I ignored it. He left voice mails asking me to let him come to my hotel room so we could talk. I guess he had asked Joe or my band guys what hotel we were staying in. I just wanted to hide from him for a while. He'd call, I'd check the voice mails as he left them, and then I just stayed in my room and cried. Then there was a knock on my door, and I didn't want to answer it. If he knew for certain that I was actually in the room, I knew he'd never leave, so I was as quiet as I could be.

I wouldn't call his behavior that night abnormal or irrational, given that he didn't have all of the facts. Had he known my secret and I'd asked him to give me space, I'm confident he would have. But as far as he understood it, I was the woman he loved, and I was with him. There were no obvious reasons why it should be breaking down, so he was fighting to save something he cared about. I'm not sure if he knew without a doubt that I actually was in that hotel room, but he said through the door, "I'm not leaving this door until you let me in." So he sat out there in the hallway by my door for over an hour. I quietly called my tour manager, Joe, and asked him if he'd come to the hall-way and somehow convince Brad to just give up for the night and try to get some sleep too. Joe did that for me with no ques-tions asked. None of that would have had to happen if I'd just been courageous enough to live my life honestly. Again, I was too afraid.

That kind of push and pull continued between Brad and me. I was driving him crazy with my erratic behavior, and our relation-ship finally started to come undone.

Shortly after the ordeal in L.A., my band and I had a midnight bus call from the Wal-Mart parking lot on Charlotte Pike just outside of Nashville. I'm not sure where we were headed. Brad and his guys had that weekend off.

He had been calling me all day long and I had not called him back. In a couple of his messages, he mentioned that he knew I was leaving that night for a show the next day and said he wanted to ride along with me so we could talk. I was ready to get away for a couple of days, alone. I arrived at bus call at about 11:45 p.m. I was in the back lounge putting my things away when Brad walked in. I was dumbfounded as to how he knew exactly when bus call was that night. He said that Joe Keiser, my production manager, had told him.

We started to talk in the back of the bus and I told him flat out that he was not going with me. He dug his heels in and said he was. I was angry with him for forcing the issue and he was angry with me for shutting him out. He started to get loud and that freaked me out. In all my years on the road, my band and crew had never seen or heard any kind of drama from me, and I cer-tainly didn't want them to hear us back there arguing. I told

Brad that I was through talking. He just wouldn't stop. I suggested we go out to the parking lot to wrap up our conversation.

As we walked through the front lounge of the bus, all of my guys were up there and they just stared at the floor. They knew something was going on and that it wasn't good. I have always been proud of not being late or causing my driver to have to sit around and wait on me. That night, my driver sat patiently and waited for me until 12:30. At that time, Brad and I were in his truck and I finally told him that I had to go. I got on the bus and walked back to the bunk area, not making eye contact with anyone, but I could feel them all looking at me. We were pulling out of the parking lot and I felt the bus stop for a second. I heard the door to the bus open and close. I looked up the hallway and there, on one of the front couches, sat Brad, with his arms crossed and his face red with frustration. I guessed he was going along for the weekend after all.

It was stressful and I tried everything I could, except the truth, to get him to see that this was not going to work out. The way he saw it was that I lacked trust in him or that I didn't really believe in love. My parents had divorced a few years earlier, and I tried to use the demise of their relationship in my strategy. I played the pessimist and agreed with him that I just didn't believe that love could last forever and that I was not a person he'd want to invest his heart in. This just sent him further into warrior mode. He was going to be the one to not let me down. He told me that he wanted to make me a promise of forever, that he wanted me to be his wife . . . whenever I was ready.

When we arrived back in Nashville early that next Monday morning, I got in my car and headed straight home. I had to completely disconnect from him. He asked if he could see me later that day. I told him no. A couple of hours later my phone started to ring. He began to leave messages again. He was crying, hurt and confused. He was at my front door, but I refused to let him in. I went upstairs, turned on some music so I couldn't hear the doorbell or the phone, and took a long bath. He was still outside in his truck. Waiting.

Brad called my friends, asking why I wouldn't talk to him. A couple of his friends would plead with me to just call him. They told me that it was killing him and that they'd never seen him like that. I didn't doubt these things, but there was no way that I could explain it to him, in truth. I felt I had no choice but to do it the way I did it.

There was nothing about Brad's behavior in the course of our relationship that was inappropriate. Yes, he was overzealous at times and a bit relentless in certain situations, but he was never out of line. I had been cruel to Brad, and I have cried a million tears about how I hurt him. I have not been ashamed of myself often, but I am ashamed of myself for choosing to be so cruel to another human being. Brad and I have seen each other in passing on a couple of occasions since then, and we exchanged pleasantries. Perhaps this book and my coming out will help him understand that time in our lives.

Casualties

Lying and hiding cause so much pain. Brad was not the first man that I'd hurt in this way. The circumstances were different with Brad, though, because we were intimate, which made me feel so much more responsible.

But there have been other men, with whom I simply wanted to share a friendship or work together, who developed feelings for me that I just couldn't reciprocate. This was confusing for them and caused a great deal of hurt.

Occasionally, these men would confess their feelings to me. I know it wasn't easy for them, and each time it happened, my heart was crushed too. I didn't want to lose the friendship. I couldn't say to them, "Oh . . . no, I'm sorry, there's been a misunderstanding. I love you as a friend, but I will never be able to love you as a lover." Had I felt able to tell the truth, I think it would have answered so many questions and freed them. I appeared available to them. They thought that I was a single woman who just hadn't found the right man and I was waiting to be loved.

I'd tell them that if they had feelings for me it would ultimately damage our friendship. I'd feel trapped and pull away in an attempt to spare their feelings. This behavior likely caused them to see me a little differently. Perhaps they titled me a bad friend, flaky, unreliable, and cold.

I hate that I forced some wonderful men in my life to believe those things to be true about me. I wanted more than anything to be a loyal and dedicated friend, through thick and thin. I have certainly needed them in my life long after I had to push them out. People like me feel trapped and forced into doing things that don't make sense to others—or to themselves, for that matter.

Try, Try Again

Julia had heard the rumors that Brad and I were seeing each other, and while she did make comments about the rumor, she never came right out and asked me if it was true.

After I cut Brad out of my life, I waited a while before I told Julia the truth about what had been going on between Brad and me. Even though I had ended things with him, I wasn't certain that I wanted to be with Julia, unless a lot of things changed.

I spent a couple of weeks trying to figure out what to do. I decided that I wanted to work things out with Julia, so I told her everything. I suppose I could have gotten away with not telling her, but I wanted something more for us. She was angry and hurt, and we had long discussions about what to do. After a week of emotional upheaval, we decided that we were worth fighting for and began couples therapy. The irony of this wasn't lost on either of us. We knew our problems stemmed largely from the fact that we couldn't find a way to publicly be a couple, so our ability to solve our difficulties with the help of a therapist was limited.

Beautiful People

J
ulia and I were feeling the benefits from our counseling, and we grew closer and healthier than we'd ever been. We were learning healthier ways to communicate our feelings to each other and how to actually hear what the other person was saying. Unfortunately, the necessity of living in the closet continued to be a strain.

Our careers progressed along successful paths, and we both worked hard.

I was in Nashville during another industry event, doing interviews. The Country Radio Seminar is one of the most hectic and exhausting weeks of the year if you're a country music artist, but I was always up for it. That five-day event was about stamina, a good attitude, and the willingness to do whatever was asked by the record label. I had been doing live interviews all morning long and had a short, twenty-minute break before my afternoon of scheduled press was to begin. My record label had a hotel room suite for all of its artists to use for the week, and I went into the bathroom to freshen up my mascara and my lipstick.

I could hear a lot of commotion outside the door. I was being escorted that day, in typical fashion, by several people—my day-to-day manager, two label executives, and the label publicist—and the conversations became loud and boisterous at times.

I could hear them outside the bathroom, but I couldn't quite make out what they were saying, nor could I determine what the tone of the conversation was. I didn't know if they were upset or excited; I just knew that everyone was talking loudly on top of one another. They had been behaving strangely for the past couple of hours.

Earlier in the day, as I was doing an interview, I had heard them in the hallway discussing something. Usually they never left my side when I was in an interview. I thought I heard one of them say, "No, we can't tell her now." I got scared. I thought there was a good chance that the label had discovered my secret and that they were going to break the news to me that everyone knew I was gay.

The anxiety washed over me, leaving me flushed and sweaty. I walked out of the bathroom and their chatter was immediately silenced. They looked at me and then down at the floor. No one would make eye contact, so I pretended that I didn't notice they were keeping something from me. I calmly announced that I was ready to head back out and wrap up the day. My label publicist, Leslie Kellner, said, "Okay, but before you go, we need to talk to you about something." I swallowed hard and said, "Okay."

I did a quick rehearsal in my head about how I would need to respond. I needed to seem unaffected, yet I wanted to have a quick response of denial. I hoped that they didn't ask me the direct question "Are you gay?" because I hated to lie about anything, and at that point I'd never had to flat-out lie about it.

"Oh, I've heard that rumor too . . . for years," I would say, to dismiss their inquiry and make sure that they saw how a stupid rumor like that couldn't rattle me. There was sweat on my top lip. I felt light-headed.

The secret they'd been keeping from me was that I'd been chosen as one of *People* magazine's 50 Most Beautiful People of the Year. I'd be going to New York for a secret photo shoot,

*It was always neat to see myself in
magazines and on television. It was a sign
that my music was being noticed. 2001.*

and no one could know about it until we were given the green
light.

Before we walked out of that hotel suite, Leslie explained that
no one was to be told this good news because *People* magazine never revealed the 50 Most Beautiful until the issue hit the
newsstands. Everyone in the room had to swear to keep quiet.
Leslie turned to me and said, "Chely, can you keep this a
secret?"

I said, "Oh, yes, I can keep a secret."

Mice Don't Speak

One of the best family vacations I ever had was back in the year 2001. I had recorded a song for Disney called "Part of Your World" for the movie *The Little Mermaid II*. Shortly after the movie came out, the folks at Disney asked me if I would travel down to Florida to be their guest of honor in a parade and to participate in a ceremony where I'd put my handprint in cement for the Disney World Walk of Fame. I declined their invitation.

I had only a five-day block of free time on my schedule for the rest of the year, and all I planned to do was stay home and have some much-needed time with Julia. Furthermore, if I decided to travel at all during my break—and that was a big "if"—Julia and I would probably go to a cabin in the mountains of Tennessee and do some hiking.

My manager, Mark, passed along my sentiments to Disney that my free time was limited and I'd be dedicating what little of it I had to my family. With that in mind, Disney suggested I bring a couple of members of my family along with me. I asked Mark to decline again. How would I ever be able to choose which family members to invite and which ones wouldn't get an invitation? At that time I had two married siblings, two nieces, and a nephew. I also knew that if I were to take my family on vacation, I wouldn't be able to take Julia. For years, I'd often been challenged with trying to figure out a way to include my partner in a family vacation without prompting my family to say, "Why is your friend invited?"

The Disney people in communication with Mark asked again why I was passing on their invitation. Disney was not giving up. They said I could bring my entire family for one week. Flights, hotels, meals—they would cover everything.

And to make sure that I felt well taken care of for my public appearances and autograph signings while I was there, Disney extended an invitation for me to bring Mark, his wife, and their children. How could I say no to that? I made the decision to go. It meant giving up my time with Julia. She wasn't upset with me for choosing to go; she understood what a treat it would be for the kids. Nevertheless, we were both disappointed to be the ones slighted—again.

I had only a couple of obligations during the week at Disney World. I was happy that the events were lumped into one day, for it meant I needed to get into hair and makeup only once during my stay.

As I sat in front of the mirror in the bathroom of my suite at the Wilderness Lodge, my two little nieces, Mandy and Erika, sat with me; they liked to see how I got all fixed up. One of my nieces asked me what exactly was going to happen in the parade, and I told her that the loudspeakers in the park would be playing my songs as the progression of cars, dancers, and characters wound slowly through the park. I told the girls that I would be riding in a convertible car with Mickey Mouse. One of the girls exclaimed, "You KNOW Mickey Mouse?!"

My family stayed with me in the staging area of the park until about ten minutes before the start of the parade because the kids wanted to meet Mickey. Our escort, Darrell, and his team had set aside a couple of minutes for my nieces and nephew to have a private meeting and photos taken with the famous rodent. I knew that the moment was nearing when I heard a couple of walkie-talkies crackling and beeping while omniscient voices announced, "Mickey is one minute away." I thought that Mandy, Erika, and Max were going to explode.

A wooden gate slowly swung in toward us and there appeared one Disney employee and one mouse, standing about seven feet tall. The kids were as thrilled as we thought they'd be, but the big surprise was that all of the adults in our group suddenly became eight years old. My heart skipped a beat, Jeny's eyes grew very wide, Chris stuck out his hand to eagerly shake with Mickey,

I was the guest of honor in a parade at Disney World. My family and I spent a week there, and meeting Mickey Mouse was the highlight for all of us. 2001.

telling him what an honor it was to finally meet him. Karla and Mike followed suit, clearly excited to meet the character that for our entire lives had represented all things magical.

Mickey and I were put into our convertible and the parade was under way. I tried my best to talk to Mickey as we rode along together and waved to the crowds who had gathered. Mickey didn't say one word to me—mice don't speak. Mickey just kept hugging me and patting me on the back and waving to the little kids, and the big kids. I was starstruck.

We arrived at the stage that had been built for the ceremony and found hundreds of fans eagerly awaiting us. Mickey took my hand and escorted me up onto the stage, where I'd be leaving my handprint in a square of fresh cement. A couple of Disney executives gave short speeches about me, my career accomplishments, and my participation in *The Little Mermaid II.* They also recognized my family and guests from the stage and said it was a thrill for Disney to be able to host them for a week of Disney Magic. I said a few thank-you's and pressed one of my hands into the wet cement. I was given some kind of pen and etched my name under my handprint.

During most of my life, my dad had been a concrete and cement worker. He regularly recruited the three of us kids, and my mom as well, to help him pour patios, sidewalks, and foundations. We were always strictly prohibited from putting a handprint or footprint into the wet, gray goop—and we wouldn't dare write our name in it. But it had always been so tempting.

I was having a surreal experience at the Wonderful World of Disney—being with Mickey Mouse and being invited and encouraged to put my hand into a slab of fresh, perfect concrete and write my name in it as fans cheered.

I wondered whether, if the world had known that I was gay, I would have been there as a guest of Disney and Mickey Mouse? It's my understanding that Disney is a very progressive corporation when it comes to the LGBT community. I believe that it has led the way in corporate America, as far as fairness and equality go with its employees. Even though I know that to be true about Disney, if I had been forthright about my sexuality within country music, would I have had the chance to become a public figure? Would I have had the chance to establish my name or my place in the entertainment world at all? Would Disney have invited me to sing for one of its movies?

From Sea to Shining Sea

After the events of September 11, 2001, I can't say that my trips to see the troops increased in frequency, but they certainly increased in intensity. I continued to dedicate at least a couple of weeks out of every year to playing for those in uniform.

In June 2003, I was asked by the USO to be a part of the biggest entertainment tour abroad in the history of the organization. The major U.S. military action into Iraq had begun in the very early months of that year, and I, along with the rest of the world, watched with great concern and worry. I was particularly on edge, because my brother, Chris, was there. He'd gone in with the early waves of troops and was in the thick of it.

At that time, Chris was a crew chief on one of the Marine Corps' most utilized helicopters, the CH-53. The Sea Stallion, as it is commonly known, is the largest single-rotor helicopter in the U.S. military's inventory. Chris's wife, Karla, had moved from Yuma, Arizona, back to the Kansas City area with their daughters shortly after he was deployed. Her family was there, and our family, for the most part, is there too. Karla and I were on the phone with each other nearly every day. Sometimes we didn't actually speak. We'd just sit there, phones to our respective ears, watching CNN like hawks.

Occasionally, an e-mail from Chris would pop into my in-box

and my heart would skip a beat. It was really too much to process that my brother was not simply on a training mission as usual—he was in a war. He'd been in the Marine Corps since 1990, and I'd become accustomed to his flying around to global destinations, but never in a war zone. His e-mails were cryptic in nature, and I was never really sure where he was or what he was doing, but I was able to determine that he was exhausted and he was in danger.

When the USO asked me to do the tour that would travel into Kuwait and Iraq, I said yes. None of the entertainers except Kid Rock would be taking their entire band and crew. I took just my tour manager, Jan Volz, Judy Seale, and my guitar player, Bruce Wallace.

In addition to music artists, there were professional athletes and movie stars. Kid Rock, Gary Sinise, Jesse James, John Stamos, Rebecca Romijn, Jason Taylor, Duce Staley, Wayne Newton, Nappy Roots, Alyssa Milano, and Brittany Murphy, to name a few. It was quite an undertaking, as there were well over a hundred people in the entourage.

We flew from our respective locations to Washington, D.C., so we could get on one plane together and go. The USO had chartered a plane from United Airlines, but it was nothing like a commercial flight. Instead, the trip over felt more like a huge tour bus, with the drinks flowing, people up walking around during takeoff and landing, and a few people in the very back smoking skinny cigarettes and cigars. I suppose they were all thinking they'd live it up one more time, because in Kuwait alcohol is illegal, and it's prohibited on military bases in Iraq.

We stopped in Amsterdam to refuel, then quickly headed off to Kuwait City. That would be our home base for the next seven days. Although Kuwait and Iraq are neighboring countries, the quality of life is markedly different. They're both oil-rich nations, but the wealth is much more evenly distributed in Kuwait. In many ways, Kuwait City looks like any American city

*My brother, Chris, was with me when I played a concert in Iwakuni,
Japan, for the Marines in 2002. He accompanied me to a press conference
and answered a couple of questions the journalists had for him.*

on any coast, bustling with resort hotels, shopping centers, and
restaurants.

Another thing Kuwait and Iraq have in common is the heat.
We landed late in the evening, and even though the sun had gone
down hours before, it was still oppressively hot. Our bags were
accounted for and word spread through the group that someone's bag had to be confiscated because there was pot in it. I
don't think that any of us fully realized the strictness of the culture that we were about to enter.

Our hotel was modern, beautifully nestled on the beach of the
Persian Gulf. The folks with the USO got us situated and sent us
off to bed. I think I finally fell asleep around four in the morning.
I'm not sure what time it was when I woke up, but it was early.
The sun was just coming up, and in the near distance I heard

chanting. It is my understanding that in the Muslim religion it is common to pray at sunrise and sunset and often there are periods of chanting. Although I was tired, I was fascinated and curious about what I was hearing. I thought there might be a mosque nearby because I could hear it so clearly. I loved how it sounded—it was serious and profound and sincere. Even the notes, in their configuration and rhythms, were foreign to me. I put my shoes on and headed out to take a look around. The chanting was coming from every direction. Almost as soon as I got outside, it ended.

I walked to the other side of the hotel, the side that faced the beach. The night before, when we had arrived, I hadn't actually seen the beach, but since I could hear it and smell it, I knew it was there. It was already about 95 degrees outside, and since I was in shorts I decided to get in the water. I kicked off my shoes and walked in up to my waist. I've always fancied it idyllic to immerse myself in bodies of water all over the world. It makes me feel connected and whole. Perhaps it prompts an old memory I have of being baptized so many years ago.

All of the artists, the journalists, and the tour coordinators were in high spirits as we boarded our buses. There was an instant camaraderie within the group, and for the most part no one expected to be treated any differently than anyone else. We were divided into about five different groups of three celebrities each. My group for the day was Alyssa Milano, Brittany Murphy, and myself. We signed autographs, shook hands, and got our pictures taken with hundreds of troops and many of the top brass too. An army captain was assigned to our group with the single task of reminding us to drink water. It was 120 degrees outside, with zero humidity, and it is common to suffer dehydration in those conditions. Our captain told us early in the day that if you start to feel thirsty it's too late. You've got to hydrate whether you think you need it or not.

The next day, before we boarded our C-130 at Camp Arifjan in Kuwait, we were each given a Kevlar helmet and a flak vest and were informed that these items would be ours for the remainder of the trip. Donning body armor to enter a war zone has a way of yanking a person into reality. It was explained to us exactly what we should do in the case of an emergency aboard our aircraft. Traveling in a military C-130 airplane is nothing like flying in a commercial aircraft—there isn't a lot of small talk because it's loud and everything seems to rattle. I positioned myself near one of the few windows in the cargo area so I could see what was below. As we approached for landing, I could see a primitive base and I noticed a large crowd of people gathered in a central location. I wondered what they were doing out there in the scorching early-afternoon sun—maybe it was some kind of training exercise. I was hopeful that some of them might be able to break away from their exercise and come say hello during our autograph session.

When we got off the plane in Tallil, Iraq, we were welcomed by the officers on the ground. In a matter of minutes, we were escorted off to wherever it was we were supposed to be. I started to hear the murmur of a crowd, and just as our group turned a corner around the tall concrete barricades, I realized that we were headed straight for the crowd I'd spotted from the air. There were hundreds of troops, standing with no tent above their heads, giving their full attention to a big stage in front of them. There was no equipment on the stage except for a sound system, and I wondered what event had just occurred.

Wayne Newton, the Dallas Cowboys Cheerleaders, and I were led into a small room behind the stage and the artists' "people" were being informed of the situation. These troops had been standing in the sun for several hours because they were told that we were coming to Tallil to put on a concert for them. The gentleman who was supposed to have done the coordination of the visits from base to base asked Wayne Newton and me what we thought we might be able to do as far as putting on a show.

Wayne and I looked at each other, amused, and responded with a laugh. We explained to him that we had no instruments, no musicians, no audio monitor engineers, and that without those things, we couldn't possibly do a show. We were concerned that the troops had been misinformed and that they'd cooked in the heat during the most dangerous part of the afternoon. The head of the USO, Ned Powell and his wife, Diane, were part of our entourage that day, and I'm sure that our tour coordinator was upset that his boss was seeing this huge mistake.

Someone went onstage and admitted the blunder to the crowd. The troops weren't angry, just disappointed. The bearer of the bad news gave them a little hope, though, by telling them that we didn't know exactly what was going to happen onstage but the performers were bound and determined to do something to entertain them.

We collectively felt that we should lead with a performance that had the best chance of winning our audience back—the Dallas Cowboys Cheerleaders. The soundman put on a CD of one of the songs that they routinely used in their shows, a high-energy dance number. The troops went crazy.

Wayne Newton happened to have a track on disc with him that was the background music for a recitation that he is known to do during his show. The soundman put on the CD over the loudspeaker and Wayne spoke his poem aloud as the track played behind him.

I, on the other hand, didn't have backing tracks. For the most part, professional country singers don't sing to tracks. I always had at least a guitar player with me, but there wasn't even a guitar onstage. Had they had a piano out there, I could have performed most any song they wanted to hear.

So, during Wayne's performance, I grabbed a couple of the low-ranking guys in uniform and asked if either of them owned a guitar. "No, ma'am," they responded in unison. I asked them if anyone on that base had a guitar. "I believe so, ma'am." I told them the situation I was in and how much it would help me out if they could locate an acoustic guitar for me. They replied, again in unison, "We're on it, ma'am."

Wayne was still onstage, and even after he'd performed his recitation, he talked to the crowd. I was hoping that there would be a guitar out there and that it would be brought to me before Wayne stepped offstage. Not that I was really that comfortable playing a guitar, I knew only a few chords, but I knew I could get by. Without a minute to spare, my guitar hunters returned with their bounty of two acoustic guitars. I pulled the first one out of its flimsy cardboard case and found it in pretty bad shape, having only four out of the usual six strings, plus it seemed the heat had left it badly warped. The second guitar had all six strings and looked as if it had one or two more songs left in it.

While Wayne wrapped up his time with the crowd, I scrounged up a pencil and a rubber band. I broke the pencil in half and used the rubber band to affix it to the neck of the guitar to function as a capo so I could play my songs in the correct keys for me to sing.

I stepped onstage just as Wayne was walking off. I imagine that from the audience it looked smooth and seamless, though it was anything but. Since I had no guitar strap and I'd have to play sitting down, I asked a soldier to walk onstage with me and bring a folding chair. Then I invited one of the men from the crowd to come up and hold the microphone for me to sing into.

I gave my disclaimer to the sand-covered crowd that I wasn't really a guitar player, but that I'd do my best. Then I sang "Shut

Up and Drive," my first hit record in country music. Much to my pleasure, a fair number of people sang along. I was the first entertainer to play and sing live for the troops in Iraq after the fall of Saddam Hussein, and I am proud of that. It wasn't a particularly good performance, but they knew that it came from my heart. After I sang, I mentioned that my brother had been right there, in Tallil, months before with his detachment of HMH-464. When I said those letters and numbers, there was a huge roar from a portion of the crowd. I don't know if they were guys assigned to HMH-464 or if they had a similar military occupational specialty, also known as their MOS. Whatever it was, their response made me feel even more connected and fortunate to be the one onstage at that moment.

The next day we did a show in Kuwait. The music artists did their thing, but the actors, comedians, models, and athletes participated onstage too.

The night before we were scheduled to fly into Baghdad, I couldn't fall asleep. I just kept imagining what it would be like. Would we really be safe? Would it look like Tallil? I did end up getting a couple hours of sleep, but was awakened again by the sunrise chanting.

Not everyone was scheduled to go into Baghdad on that day. About half of the group was to be choppered out to a U.S. aircraft carrier somewhere in the Persian Gulf. The rest of us were headed north, to Baghdad International Airport, a.k.a. BIAP. BIAP had been the Iraqis' civilian airport before the occupation, but it was now the hub of activity for the Coalition forces in the region.

I was beginning to connect with a few people on the tour and was excited that most of my new pals were the ones with whom I'd be traveling to BIAP.

I loved Jesse James, the guy who has a television show called *Monster Garage.* He was laid-back and a gentleman. Kid Rock was so easy to like too. Yes, he's a bit of a bad-boy renegade, but there is a paradox to his persona. He is a sweetheart, in tune with his fans and disciplined in many ways. I have tremendous respect for him. John Stamos and his then wife, Rebecca Romijn, were part of the tour too. They showed a great concern for the troops and gave them their undivided attention. Gary Sinise, whom I also came to know on that trip, is a patriot in every sense of the word and has become a very good friend of mine. So some of my favorite people on the tour and I put on our gear and boarded another C-130 plane.

Our pilots performed a combat landing into Baghdad due to the potential threat of insurgent fire from the ground. A combat landing is when the pilots maneuver the aircraft in random ways—up and down, side to side—to make it more difficult to

Iraq, June 2003. The quilt we are holding was made as a tribute to some of those who died in the September 11, 2001, terrorist attacks. Gary Sinise is to my right, and John Stamos is on the other side of the quilt.

shoot out of the air. This type of landing can cause a bit of a sick stomach, and since I was already nervous it really did a number on me. We were greeted on the flight line by the highest-ranking officials on the base. They quickly put us into a little bus and started driving toward a large aircraft hangar. As we stepped off the bus, the first order of business was to find the Port-A-Potties, and we scurried through a maze of concrete barriers and sandbag walls like little laboratory mice.

As soon as we gathered outside the latrine, we were informed that there was a problem. The man in charge of the tour turned to me and said, "Chely, we've got the same problem we had in Tallil. You gotta put something together quick. There are instruments onstage this time—you guys can do a show, right?" None of us had our entire bands with us. We were a bare-bones group of people who had come equipped with our black Sharpies and the intention of signing hundreds of autographs.

As we were led back through the labyrinth of concrete and sand, we concocted a plan. I said to John Stamos, "Hey, you were Uncle Jesse on that sitcom and you played guitar on the show, so you can do that, right?" He said, "No, I really don't play guitar that well." Rebecca, his wife, said, "Well he *does* play drums—he plays on tour with the Beach Boys." So John was our drummer. When we turned the corner to walk into the aircraft hangar, we were met with a wall of heat and sound. It was about 125 degrees outside, and we were told later that day that it had been more than 140 degrees inside that hangar.

There were thousands of excited, sweat-soaked men and a few women packed in the big metal building, and there wasn't an autograph table or a poster in sight. Instead, a big stage stood at the far end of the building, and we were shoved through the crowd for at least two minutes before we reached it. We didn't even have time to discuss what we were going to do up there— Kid Rock just yelled out to us, "We're gonna wing it. Let's kick some ass!"

With Kid Rock in Qatar. 2003.

John sat down behind the drum kit, called out a count, and started playing. I don't think he had a particular song in mind, he just seemed to know that we needed to make some noise. Gary Sinise grabbed the bass guitar, my guitar player and Kid Rock's guitar player each found a suitable instrument, and Kid Rock and I were the singers. We were all completely drenched with sweat before the end of the first song. If Kid Rock was singing lead, I was singing his background vocals. When I sang lead, he jumped in with a background vocal.

A couple of times during the show, someone in uniform grabbed the mic and yelled out that a certain group of guys needed to leave the audience in a hurry and go do something war-related. There were actual emergency situations that had happened while we were playing—a first for those of us onstage.

At one point, while the band was playing an instrumental break in a song, Kid Rock shouted in my ear, "Do you know the song that I did with Sheryl Crow called 'Picture'?" I told him that I'd heard it, that I knew the melody but was uncertain of the words. He said, "That's cool. We're gonna do it and I'm going to tell you your lines as they come."

The crowd's intensity never let up for the entire ninety minutes. In fact, the volume level grew. Models and professional athletes were singing background vocals, having the time of their lives. We eventually wrapped up the performance, and we all laughed when Kid Rock said, "Hey, now *that* was rock and roll!"

Back to the Desert

I returned to the Middle East a year later, this time with my entire band and crew. We didn't fly in and out of Iraq every day to the safety and comfort of a posh hotel. Once we arrived in Iraq, we stayed in Iraq. I experienced more than I ever imagined I would, and it changed my life. We had days filled with excitement and fun, but when things got heavy, the experience changed dramatically.

On September 19, 2004, one of the last few days of an eight-

I'm not sure what kind of aircraft I'm flying in,
but I'm sure it was exhilarating! Afghanistan, 2005.

day tour, we choppered into a remote camp in Iraq called FOB Summerall. At the time, the troops on the ground were a part of the Big Red One. During World War II, my grandfather, Sgt. Harold Henry, had served as part of the Big Red One, and in some way I felt I was honoring him by being there.

After the show, a young man from Apollo, Pennsylvania, introduced himself to me as Josh Henry. I got chills and informed him that my grandfather had been a member of the Big Red One and that his last name was Henry too. Two different wars, two soldiers named Henry.

The band and I stayed and visited with the soldiers at FOB Summerall until about three o'clock in the morning.

After only a few hours' sleep, we flew to Camp Taji to do the last show of the tour. When we landed, we were informed that Josh Henry had just been killed in action.

After the show, even though I was exhausted, I didn't really want to go to bed. It seemed that I wasn't alone—the band and crew weren't headed for their bunks either. Usually, when we're staying on a base, I sleep at a different location than the band and crew, because military bases determine sleeping quarters according to gender. Our sleeping arrangements that night at Taji were unusual; we were all assigned to stay in the same little building. It was the building of the chaplain's office, which felt comforting on that particular night. Before we arrived, bunks were put in a couple of the small rooms in the building. There was a short hallway that connected the bunkrooms, the bathroom, and the chaplain's office.

Once all of our equipment had been packed up after the show, the guys headed off to midnight chow, as it's called in the military. After I signed autographs, I was taken back to the bunkhouse. One by one, the rest of our group gathered there. Within a few minutes, we all ended up sitting on the concrete floor with our backs against the plywood walls, talking about how we were feeling.

The shared emotion was one of shock. We'd all been around the world together many times, and we'd experienced a lot of situations, but this was different—this was a war, a real war. It wasn't something on CNN being reported to us—we had stepped into the story itself.

As the men in my group talked openly, I heard something unfold in their discussion and it shrouded my emotions for a few minutes. I sat quietly as they talked about an element of this experience that had never occurred to me. A few admitted that they had often felt guilty for not serving their country in the military as their fathers, uncles, and grandfathers had done. My respect and understanding of how Josh's death affected them, as men, grew in great measure. We'd had so much fun and excitement on the tour, but now we had been given a much different glimpse into the lives of those who serve.

The emotional ante would be raised yet again the next morning. We were flown in Black Hawk helicopters to Baghdad International Airport, where we were to board our C-130 plane to get us out of Iraq. It's common when we fly military planes for flight schedules to be ever changing and not on time. We were supposed to wait an hour or so before our flight was to leave Baghdad, but our officer in charge continued to check in with us and tell us that it would be just a while longer. This waiting went on for a few hours.

We didn't do a lot of talking as we waited for our flight, but we did stick together in a pack. Many of us had been keeping journals during the trip, so a few of us were writing and others were taking pictures. The officer in charge of us that day was a woman. I noticed that she approached our tour manager, they had a brief conversation in the corner, and then they both walked over to our group and asked us to gather around.

The twenty-something-year-old officer told us that we were about to have the sad but honorable responsibility of being aboard an H.R. flight. She had to explain to us that "H.R."

stands for "human remains." We were given precise instructions on how to board the plane and what to do and not do during the entire flight. You could hear the collective breath knocked out of us as we listened to the officer. Her youth was juxtaposed with her solemn duty, and I could tell that not only was she emotional that a life had been lost, but she felt sorry for us that we were having this experience. After she said the words of an officer, she paused and said the words of just another person in the room. "You guys okay? I know, this sucks so bad. I'm sorry. Hang in there, you're almost out of here."

The body was loaded into the plane before any passengers could go aboard. Most of us were traveling with a backpack and a rolling computer bag, and we were instructed to avoid rolling any bags while passing by the body. They asked us to show respect by not listening to iPods or using laptop computers. We were expected to sit quietly during the flight, which we did.

There was a primitive wooden box draped with an American flag, strapped tightly to the floor at our feet. We were each buckled into a canvas seat that hung from one interior wall of the plane and from a steel divide in the center of the aircraft. Five of us on one side and five on the other, we were just six feet apart and between us was the body. The toes of my tennis shoes would have easily touched the wooden casket, but I pulled my feet back up under my seat.

As the wheels of our C-130 lifted off the paved runway, I looked around at our group and saw that not one of us was trying to hide our emotions—we were all crying.

After we landed in Kuwait, a colonel came aboard to tell us what was about to happen. Since we had picked up a few military personnel in Baghdad who were headed to Kuwait, he addressed them first. The last thing he said to them was, "Be advised that the deceased is a civilian, so it is not necessary to stand at attention." I was relieved that Josh wasn't in that casket, but on the other hand, I was also sad that it wasn't Josh.

The casket was to be removed first and we were to follow. As soon as the big back hatch of the plane was opened and lowered to the ground, I saw about twenty uniformed men and women standing quietly. A few of them hopped up into the aircraft and removed the straps that had secured the casket to the hot steel floor. Several audible commands were given and, like choreographed dancers, they picked up the wooden box and began a slow walk down the ramp. The others in uniform positioned behind the C-130 created a human corridor which connected the path of the casket to the back of a white box truck. The door of the truck was rolled up and the engine was not running. I recall noticing that despite the fact that we were on a flight line, the setting was eerily quiet.

I followed behind the small procession and took a place next

There is not a more appreciative audience in the world than our troops.
Somewhere in the Middle East. 2004. (Clay Krasner, bass guitar;
Steve Cudworth, acoustic guitar.)

to the others on the ground. Everyone in uniform was standing at full attention as the men carrying the casket lifted it and slid it into the back of the truck. Then one man climbed inside the back of the truck and pulled the door down, shutting himself inside.

Those in uniform relaxed their stance and walked away. The colonel was next to me and saw that I was crying. "Sir," I asked him, "even though you told everyone that he was a civilian and that they didn't need to stand at attention, why did they anyway?" "Ma'am, because he's an American and he's going home," he said.

In the days to come, we would learn that man in the casket was Eugene Armstrong, an American contractor who was one of several men kidnapped and beheaded in Baghdad.

I was worn out by my ten-day trip to the Middle East.

I knew I would never be the same.

Judy Seale and I had a wonderful day with the kids in a town called Balad, Iraq. Most of these kids had never attended a day of school in their lives until this school was built by the Coalition forces. We showed up with school supplies, soap, and toys. The children were excited, and my heart was stolen a thousand times that day. 2004.

My Sister, Jeny

My journey to Iraq in 2004 had affected me so profoundly that I knew it was time to come out to my sister, Jeny. I felt that I'd been given a gift in seeing, firsthand, how delicate and precious life is, and although Josh Henry and others weren't around any longer to live their lives, I was.

The moment I arrived home, I called Jeny and asked her to get in her car and head to Tennessee. After she arrived, we stayed up and talked for hours about the trip to Iraq, and she understood that it had been a life-changing experience for me. The next morning, we were sitting outside in my courtyard drinking coffee and I blurted out, "Jeny, I need to tell you something—I'm gay." I started crying. She stood up and grabbed me out of my chair and hugged me.

We talked a lot during the next couple of days. My objective was for my sister to know me. I wanted her to know about my life and from that moment on, she has.

Jeny's husband, a conservative Christian, believes homosexuality is a sin. Jeny and Mike's kids are a big part of my life, and it would devastate me if that ever changed. I wasn't willing to risk his judgment of me, so I begged Jeny not to tell him.

Mike is a wonderful person, a good father and good husband to my sister. I knew it was a lot to ask her to keep a secret from her husband, but I suppose we both felt a similar uneasiness about what his reaction might be.

Jeny is my best friend, and our friendship became even stronger once I confided in her about my sexuality. When I told her, I was surprised that she didn't say, "Chel, I knew the whole time." Instead, she told me that she'd wondered about it before but then decided otherwise. Most of all, she said that she was happy and relieved to know that I wasn't living my life alone.

Jeny and I were born fifteen months apart, and like most siblings that close in age, we fought like wild animals once we got past the ages of seven or eight. During our school years, we were quite different. She was tough and seemed self-assured and didn't need to be popular or accepted by the other kids at school like I did.

I'd confront her and ask her why she had to be so tough, why couldn't she just try to be friends with everyone. She'd tell me

Jeny and me in Santorini, Greece, in 2006.
We have a great time anywhere we go.

that I was a scared follower and would probably never stand up for myself. Prophetic, in a way, I suppose. It would take me some twenty-five years to stand up for what I believe.

After high school, we became friends again. We'd both grown up quite a bit and realized that we were lucky to have each other. I was on the road most of the time, but we talked almost every day.

In the years following my coming out to Jeny, our relationship has continued to deepen. I value the comfort of her undying friendship and unconditional love. We keep each other in check, cheer each other on, and encourage each other to become better people every day. My sister is an inspiration to me in so many ways.

A Great American

My manager informed me that Vice President Dick Cheney's office had called and asked if I would come do an event for him. I declined a couple of times. I had made it a personal policy not to participate in political events. The vice president's office assured my manager that it was not a political event, but rather a private party. The Cheneys were going to have some of the wounded and recovering troops from Walter Reed Army Medical Center and Bethesda National Naval Medical Center bused over to their residence for a poolside barbecue. Once I learned what the gathering was about, I said that I would love to be involved, and soon plans were under way for the event.

I visit Walter Reed and Bethesda frequently, so there was a good chance that I had already met a number of the folks who would be in attendance. They were invited to bring their families to the party, and I was looking forward to catching up with the loved ones as well. Often, during those bedside visits, the wounded are not conscious, or if they are, the doctors have them on so much morphine to control pain levels that they're not quite lucid. So it wasn't unusual to spend visiting time talking to a mom, a dad, a wife, or a sibling. The families with whom I've visited are steadfast and special. I was definitely eager to see them all.

The day of the show was busy. I needed to be in Nashville for meetings until two o'clock that afternoon. I arrived at the Nashville airport only to learn that my flight to D.C. was delayed due to heavy thunderstorms in the area and I was told that the storms were hitting many areas of the Northeast, including Washington. The schedule for the day was tight to begin with, but given the weather situation, I started to wonder if I'd make it to Washington at all.

My manager suggested I do my hair and makeup in the bathroom on the plane to save a little time. The folks in D.C., my manager, and I were trying to figure out a way to pull this show off. My band and crew had been at the vice president's residence all day long, setting up the production and doing sound checks, so if I could just get there on time, the show could go on.

I finally landed in Washington in an airplane that held about twenty-five passengers. I was able to get ready in the bathroom on the plane. I hadn't checked any luggage, but because the plane was so small, even the carry-on bags wouldn't fit in the cabin. The passengers, including me, stood outside the plane waiting for the crew to give us our briefcases, purses, and small duffel bags. It was raining and the area where we were instructed to stand and wait was flooded. So there I was, in full drag— ready for a performance—in just enough rain for my hair to be a wreck. I was soaked, head to toe. The drive to the vice president's residence was supposed to take about thirty minutes. I was confident that I could fix my hair and clean up my makeup while I was in the backseat of the car.

I finally got my bag and, once I entered the airport from the tarmac, was greeted by a professional military man. He introduced himself to me and said, "Miss Wright, this way. We're in quite a hurry, but we'll get you there for your show."

The rain continued to pour down, causing water to flow over some of the roads and slowing traffic to a crawl. While I was rummaging through my hair and makeup kit, I overheard the driver talking on his cell phone. The second he'd hang up from one call, his phone would ring again. I could tell there was something being coordinated that sounded urgent.

From out of nowhere came a fleet of emergency vehicles. Some appeared to be standard metro police cars, but there were also several unmarked, large black sport utility vehicles with blue lights flashing from every crack and crevice. My driver needed to pull over to make way for the vehicles. Perhaps he was distracted by his phone calls and didn't realize he needed to get over, so I told him that we should pull over and let them by. He laughed and told me that they were here for us, to escort our car to the vice president's residence.

At every exit and overpass we came upon, I could see there were several emergency vehicles at those points as well, and I realized that there had to be fifty vehicles involved in this effort. I asked my driver if this was a typical day for him. It wasn't, but when Vice President and Mrs. Cheney got word that I was stuck in traffic and might not make it to the performance, they gave the order for me to have a full escort.

The barbecue at the residence had been moved indoors due to the rain. The troops and their families had already enjoyed their hot dogs, hamburgers, and steaks and were patiently waiting for me to show up. As soon as my driver pulled up to the front door of the vice president's residence, several people just inside the building introduced themselves and began to give me the timeline of the evening's events. The Cheneys' right-hand gal informed me that Vice President and Mrs. Cheney wanted to speak with me before the performance.

I was taken to a small room that was crowded with production equipment. Once I was put in the room, my band guys and crew checked in with me. We discussed the usual pre-show details, and they gave me the information I would need for the event.

Then I was escorted to a bright, busy hallway, and less than a minute later Vice President and Mrs. Cheney greeted me. Mrs.

Cheney was friendly, thanking me repeatedly for agreeing to come play for the troops, and then the vice president made a lighthearted comment about how happy he was that his people were able to get me through the crazy weather and traffic situation outside. He laughed and suggested that a disaster had been averted because the wounded troops certainly didn't want to hear him sing. All the while, the official photographer continued to snap photos of us as Vice President Cheney asked me about my trips to the Middle East. He also mentioned that he knew my brother, Chris, was a Marine who'd served in Iraq and Kuwait. "Tell him hi and thank you, will ya?" he said.

I don't care who you are, when you're engaged in a conversation with the second-most-powerful man in the world, it's notable. Regardless of what I thought about his judgment, his decisions, or his policies, he has a commanding presence that is undeniable. I was having visions of my great inquisition of the vice president. At the same time, I was noticing the pattern of his speech and the way his top lip curved upward on one side. I was being forced to exercise mild amounts of restraint to fight off the urge to spill my inappropriate rant. I wanted to say, "Mr. Vice President, I have questions about KBR. I have questions about interrogation of prisoners. I want to know how you can sleep at night knowing that the policies that your party creates and supports deny so many people their basic freedoms. AND—your daughter is GAY, for God's sake. What are you thinking?!"

He asked me a question that required a direct answer. I felt a twinge of arrogance and excitement, because the answer to his question required specific knowledge of a particular military base and its proximity to a border, and I was ready to deliver my clever response. Just as he punctuated the inquiry with his vocal inflection and the lifting of the one eyebrow, I had the answer beautifully formed in my head, ready to pass through my lips.

Suddenly I felt an odd sensation on my right foot. I had to

look down, breaking contact with the vice president to see what was going on.

The worst had happened. The entire front half of my boot had exploded and my size 11 foot, covered in its white athletic sponge of a sock, had slid out of the boot at least two inches. Once I had stepped off the airplane, I had been forced to stand in that deep puddle of rainwater and my black patent leather boots were soaked. Because my duffel bag had been out of reach on the plane, I couldn't put on my black dress socks, which would've been more comfortable to wear with those delicate boots and wouldn't have sopped up all of that water. Instead I had to continue wearing the thick socks that I'd had on with my other shoes.

There was actually a tiny puddle of water on the floor. I knew that I couldn't just ignore my exploded boot. Even if I could sneak away without anyone noticing that my big white foot was not in my boot, I couldn't allow a puddle of water to be standing on a marble floor in a hallway that was being traveled by wounded and recovering men and women, men and women who were learning to get around on crutches and new prosthetic limbs. I couldn't do that.

I directed the Cheneys' attention to my boot and said, "Mr. Vice President, Mrs. Cheney, it seems as though my boot has exploded." They quickly looked and they both said, at the exact same time, "Wow!" Mrs. Cheney asked if there was anything she could do to help and even offered to have someone go retrieve a pair of her boots for me to wear. I laughed and told her that I wear a size 11 shoe. She exclaimed, "Oh, my!" I excused myself and sent someone to ask Rookie, my production manager, to meet me back in that little room behind the stage. When he arrived I told him that I had a wardrobe emergency and that I needed him to get a roll of gaff tape. "Sure thing, Chief."

After I dried everything as best I could, Rookie and I propped my foot up on a rolling anvil case and wrapped my boot all the way around until there was no leather showing. Just a boot made of black gaff tape.

The crowd was eager to begin and so was I. The Cheneys gave me a beautiful introduction and I took the stage. After my second song, I glanced over about six feet to my right, where the vice president and his wife were sitting attentively, and caught them both staring at my boot. They quickly looked up at me and each gave me the thumbs-up. Vice President Cheney mouthed the words "Looks good." I shared the story with the crowd and summed it up by thanking the vice president for acting as my wardrobe consultant.

It was an amazing night. My favorite part was signing autographs and visiting after the performance with the troops and their families. There was even a Marine in attendance whom I had met just hours after he'd been severely wounded in Bagh-

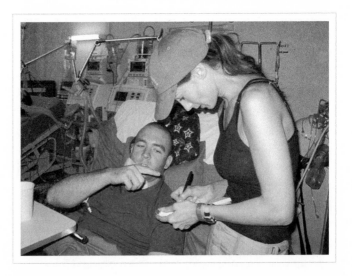

During one of my trips to Baghdad, in 2004, I met this young Marine named Jake. We still e-mail each other from time to time.

dad. We hadn't met on a base, but rather in a hospital in the center of Baghdad where the Coalition forces had set up shop. On the afternoon we met, we were both scared to death—it was nice to be with him again, in a vastly different circumstance.

I stayed in D.C. that night and struggled to fall asleep. I was tired, but my mind raced with the details of such a crazy yet fulfilling day. I thought for a long time about the vice president and how I could make all of the pieces of my experience with him fit. I still had fundamental differences with him on a number of levels, but now I'd had this fun, quirky interpersonal exchange with him that was lighthearted. He was charming, funny, polite, and appreciative of my relationship with the troops.

Then I thought about the things he said to the audience before I took the stage. He called me an "all-American gal from the heartland" whose family had a long history of military service. And once again I was called a "good American." I thought of Mary, the Cheneys' daughter. Her father, one of the most powerful political figures in the world, aligns himself with and is a leader in the Republican Party—the very group of people who collectively denounce homosexuals and suggest that we are a tear in the moral fabric of society. They are the very party that leads the fight to prohibit any policy that would allow real equality and freedom. Furthermore, Vice President Cheney's party actively seeks to create new laws and legislation that specifically deny equality and protection for gays.

Although Dick Cheney has stated his support for his daughter and his opinion that "people ought to be free to enter into any kind of relationship they want to," I am less than moved. In fact, I feel that his words are halfhearted and insulting—not to mention a day late and a dollar short. For the most part, he kept quiet about the topic during the years when he could have been most effective for change. He failed to use his power to do the right thing.

"Historically," he said, "the way marriage has been regulated is at the state level." C'mon, Dick, we all know that this is a cop-out. We all know that sometimes the states cannot be relied upon to make decisions like that—creating legislation that is fair and constitutional in a timely fashion.

Surely it hasn't slipped Mr. Cheney's mind that the U.S. Supreme Court had to intervene to make interracial marriage legal in all fifty states back in 1967. Had it been left to the states to decide, it wouldn't have happened—and if it ever did, I wouldn't have seen it in my lifetime.

In 1958 Mildred and Richard Loving (a black woman and a white man) had been arrested and criminally charged under a Virginia state statute that banned interracial unions.

Robert F. Kennedy, the attorney general at the time, stepped in and referred the Lovings to the American Civil Liberties Union. The ACLU, on the Lovings' behalf, presented their complaint to the Virginia Supreme Court of Appeals. The result: the criminal convictions of the Lovings leveled by the Commonwealth of Virginia were upheld—they were still not allowed to legally reside in their home state and were sentenced to a year in prison, which was suspended for twenty-five years on the condition that they leave the state. The state of Virginia had the chance to recognize that a statute written in 1924 was unconstitutional, but in its wise statehood, it upheld the archaic law.

The ACLU and the Lovings appealed to the U.S. Supreme Court, which finally overturned their convictions and ruled that the state of Virginia's statute was unconstitutional. The rest is history.

So, in my opinion, Vice President Cheney's stance that "states should decide" is hollow. It's merely a way to placate his daughter and those of us who believe that gay marriage should be mandated at the federal level and that anything short of that is unconstitutional.

·   ·   ·

I had not come out to my father yet, but I cried as I lay on the bed that night in a Washington, D.C., hotel room. I thought about how hard it would be to have my dad behave like Vice President Cheney if I ever did have the courage to tell him that I'm gay. I imagined what it would feel like to be Mary. If my dad were ever the second-most-powerful man in the world and he could do something to preserve and establish my rights of equality but instead chose to pass the buck, I would be really hurt and disappointed.

At a National Press Club gathering in 2009, Mr. Cheney said, "As many of you know, one of my daughters is gay, and it is something we have lived with for a long time in our family."

It's not cancer. It's not drug addiction. It's not domestic abuse.

There in my hotel room, I realized that just hours before, I had stood with the vice president of the United States and wished that he were something he wasn't. The irony is, if he had known who I am, he'd probably have wished the same about me.

Steel on Steel:
Master Sergeant Wright

So often, people ask me about my brother and his service in the military. I'm incredibly impressed and proud of all that he's accomplished. But sometimes, I can't help but think of him as a little boy—that's when I knew him best. Chris was a fifth grader and had been coming home from school with bumps and bruises and sometimes a low-hung head. When my folks asked Chris who'd been picking on him, he told them the name of the boy: Matt Collier. My parents demanded that my brother stick up for himself and tell that boy and any other boy that might give him a hard time to back off or else. I'm not sure if Chris attempted the suggested two-party talks with Matt, but a day or so later, my brother came trudging down the sidewalk once again with the telltale signs of another school yard rumble that hadn't gone his way. Later that evening, my dad arrived home from work and stepped into the chaos that met him every single time he walked through the door. He was usually greeted by my mother's harsh recap of what one, both, or all of us kids had done, and she'd often follow with the question, "What are *you* going to do about it?" In the few seconds it took for him to throw his Botsford Ready Mix ball cap to the floor and commence a defeated, exaggerated expulsion of air—perhaps trying to force from his skull what must have been a decade-long headache from which I knew both of my parents to suffer—my mom told my dad *exactly* what he was going to do about it.

In this instance, in regards to my brother getting roughed up at school again, my mom had come up with a dandy of a plan, which my father followed to the letter. Mom stayed in the kitchen and smoked cigarettes, while Jeny and I went to the front porch. Within minutes, my dad and my brother both got into the cab of the pickup truck, backed out of the driveway onto Main Street, and slowly pulled away.

Not quite an hour later, just after the sky had stopped bouncing pinks and purples around, the truck barreled into the driveway and skidded to a halt. Dad got out and slammed his door. He didn't go into the house. I think he went directly to the dog kennels that were in the far backyard. I wasn't sure that Chris was even in the truck until I heard the creaking of steel on steel as he opened his door. I was watching him from the side porch and wondered why he wasn't getting out. Finally, I saw him exit the truck.

I don't know where our mother had gone, but Jeny and I stood together as Chris came through the screen door and walked into the glow of a single fluorescent light that hung above the kitchen sink. He was bloody. Real bloody. He was dirty too, and his short-sleeved plaid shirt was missing its top couple of buttons. I didn't recognize the look of his face. At least one of his eyes was already swollen. I don't remember if it was his top lip or lower lip that was split open, but one of them looked like ground round. He was crying. My big brother, whom I'd always known to be pretty emotionally static, was making noises that sounded like a dog who'd been hit by a car.

Jeny and I were crying too, but we immediately snapped into action. We sat Chris down in the back part of the kitchen while he mumbled in a stupor, trying to tell us what happened and that he'd "gotten in a couple of good licks too" on our father. My sister and I got butter knives, stood on a chair, and chipped ice from the inside walls of the freezer. We harvested enough to put into dish towels and gently placed our two homemade ice packs on our combat buddy's face.

In the days that followed, we learned that our father was instructed by our mother to take their son to a cornfield and beat him up. To teach him how to fight. So he wouldn't be a *sissy*. He was eleven.

God only knows if the plan to de-sissify my brother by beating him like that could have been successful, but Jeny and I decided to take matters into our own hands. We plotted for a couple of days and then put our own plan into action.

We staked out our victim after school, and then we ambushed. My sister and I jumped Matt Collier when he was all alone, knocked him down, took our shoes off, and beat him from head to toe, while warning him never, ever to touch our brother again. It worked.

Don't Ask, Don't Tell

I have been given awards for work that I have done on behalf of our troops, public school children, and other groups of people in need. Although these awards and titles were certainly not necessary, I am proud of them.

I have been named Kansan of the Year and the American Legion's Woman of the Year. I have received the FAME Award from the Music Educators National Conference in Washington, D.C., and numerous other accolades. Typically, before I walk up onstage to accept an award, someone reads a prepared speech that highlights reasons why they have chosen to honor me. More often than not, at some point in the speech, the declaration is made: "Chely Wright is a great person and a fine American."

If those people reading their speeches knew that I am a gay woman, would they say that about me? I doubt that Vice President Dick Cheney and Mrs. Cheney would have invited me to their home in Washington, D.C., to entertain. I doubt that I would have been invited by President and Mrs. Bush to sing before our commander in chief took the stage for a speech in Seoul, South Korea. I wonder, if the world had known that I was gay, would I have been invited to be the grand marshal of the Veterans Day Parade in New York City? If I were known to be a gay woman, would I have ever been invited to do the things for the community and the troops in the first place? Maybe not. The "maybe not" has held me back my entire life.

I am still in contact with men and women I have met while on tour to perform for the troops. I have sat in foreign and domestic military dining facilities, fitness centers, and makeshift lounges with these folks as they show me pictures they keep in their wallets. Pictures tattered by miles and faded by sweat.

There are often newer pictures that find their place in the pile of memories—a photo of a new baby or a snapshot from a wedding that happened back home during leave. I have watched these families grow; in some cases, I've watched them fall apart. Deployment is hard on families.

There are many stereotypes about people in the military. I have met troops who are blue-collar-type guys and gals and I know our military simply could not function without their hard work and specific areas of training. On the other hand, I've met folks who graduated from major universities and colleges with degrees in math, science, literature, medicine—you name it— and they are in our U.S. military. Our service personnel represent a cross section of society just like any other group of people does. They are individuals, each to be understood and recognized.

There is a specific group of men and women in the armed services, however, who are not recognized. Not only are they not recognized, they are ignored. The gays who serve our country are forced to endure and participate in the "don't ask, don't tell" policy. It is a ridiculous charade. We're all taught at a young age that telling half-truths is lying and that lies by omission are still lies. Our government endorses, encourages, and requires such lies.

The military places a high value on honor, integrity, honesty, and valor. The policy of "don't ask, don't tell" seems to be the antithesis of those ideals. Often, when I've spent time with troops, I've gotten a sense that I'm speaking with a gay service member. I just want to hug that person and whisper in his or her ear, "You are like me and I am like you."

While their straight comrades get the luxury of saying out loud that they are homesick for their wife, their girlfriend, their husband, or their boyfriend, gay service members are mandated to keep quiet. If their partner has a car wreck and dies back home while they're deployed, they don't get to go home. Gay service members endure the same hardships, but are forced to keep their mouths shut or lose their career.

The point in this policy, as I understand it, is that the policy-makers believe that gays won't be able to serve with same-sex troops without wanting to have sexual intercourse with them, so

Having the chance to learn about the guys and gals in uniform and what their day-to-day lives are like is my favorite part of going to see the troops. This young man (part of a Stryker Brigade) was telling me about having been in a fierce battle just weeks before. 2004.

it's best to not declare sexuality. That makes no sense to me. I am gay. I am attracted to women, but not all women. Homosexuality does not make a person promiscuous, perverted, unprofessional, or without judgment.

Once I tell the world that I am a lesbian, I wonder if I will be invited back or welcomed to entertain the troops.

Hannity and Wright

In 2003, just days after I returned from my first trip into Iraq, I wrote a song called "Bumper of My S.U.V." It was inspired by a real incident in which another driver flipped me off when she saw the Marine Corps bumper sticker on my car. The song wasn't meant as a political ballad but a statement from my heart: it's important to honor those who serve.

Although I hadn't released "Bumper of My S.U.V." to radio on a record label, fans of country music—many of them in the military or with family members in the service—loved the song. The record got played on radio stations around the country, and reached #1 on the Billboard singles chart. Its success surprised me, but the reaction of some on the political right surprised me even more. The song was never intended to be out on the airwaves and it was certainly never meant to be an endorsement of the Iraq war or the policies of the Bush administration. But that's not how some heard it.

When "Bumper of My S.U.V." became a hit record, not only was it being played on radio stations of all genres, but it created quite a stir in the media as well. This accidental hit record was plainly and simply a phenomenon.

One of the many calls that came in was from Fox's *Sean Hannity Show.* I was asked if I would come to New York and be on the show.

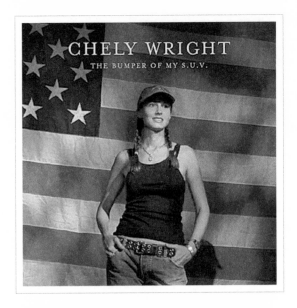

*My good friend Jan Volz snapped this photograph of me
after sound check in front of a really big, genuine cloth
American flag that hung on a base in Kuwait. It would
later become the cover for the CD single of the song
"Bumper of My S.U.V." 2004.*

Since Sean had invited me, and many other television and
radio shows were also requesting that I appear on their programs, I headed to New York for a week of press. I was happy to
share stories of my trips to see the troops, which was the focus of
all of the interviews.

I love to do interviews. I'm not into giving an answer that will
cause an awkward moment on the air just for the sake of being
adversarial; some people are into shock value, but I am not. Nevertheless, I do my best to be contemplative and honest when I'm
asked a question.

I was looking forward to being on Sean Hannity's show. Most

everyone knows that he has a television program on the Fox News Channel, but he also has a popular syndicated radio program. I was told that I'd be on with him for most of that day's radio show, and I was hopeful that we'd be able to cover a lot of ground. I had so much I wanted to share about my most recent trip to the Middle East and the song "Bumper of My S.U.V."

My fan club and Web site were being deluged with letters from people who had heard the song. They were sharing with me personal, detailed, and emotional stories of what the song meant to them and how it was affecting their lives. The response was overwhelming, and I was looking forward to sharing the experience with Sean and his listeners. Although Sean's show has a talk-show format, he had been playing my record for a couple of weeks and had shared with me before my trip to New York that it was a smash and was definitely resonating with his listeners. This is the perfect way to walk into a radio interview—with a hit record, a supportive host, and a fan base that wants to hear the story. Sean was charming, had his facts and figures correct, and did what a cream-of-the-crop journalist does—he informs and entertains.

During the first few segments of the show, we discussed my family's military history, my many trips overseas, and how the song "Bumper of My S.U.V." came to be written. We also talked about how the song eventually got recorded and how it ended up being played on the radio. He praised the song and went on and on about how he'd never played a record on his show before that had lit up the phone lines the way my song did. I was touched by his compliments about my time spent with the troops and his genuine admiration for the song.

We took calls live on the air from his listeners, who had been jamming the phone lines. I recall that a couple of the callers who actually got through were guys that I'd performed for while they were deployed.

Then it was time for a commercial break. While the advertisements ran, Sean and I continued to talk and share stories. He mentioned to me that he hosts an annual event called the Hannity Freedom Concerts and suggested that I come play at one of the shows. He had hosted the event for a few years, and he was now having several concerts across the nation. He said that his audience loved "Bumper of My S.U.V." so much when he played it on his radio program that it would be a thrill for them if I were able to come sing it live at his Freedom Concert. I said that I would love to be a part of his concert event.

We came back from the commercial break and Sean said something to the effect of my being a "good conservative, Republican country music singer." I laughed and corrected him, saying that I was not a Republican, and he seemed shocked. He asked me if I was a supporter of George W. Bush. I explained to him that I was, indeed, in support of George Bush—because Bush was the president of the United States and whether or not I voted for him was irrelevant. My point was that since he was, at that time, the president, I was in support of him but that I didn't necessarily agree with all of his policies.

Live on the radio, I told Sean that I had a couple of pretty significant problems with George W. Bush. Sean asked me specifically what those problems were. He only gave me a chance to talk about one of my issues with the president, and I'm glad that I led with the one I did. I told him that I thought the fact that the president allows gays to be discriminated against in the process of adopting children is disgraceful. And that I thought the policy of leaving such matters for individual states to decide is passive-aggressive, negligent, and transparently hateful. I went on to tell Sean that I liken the president's stance to that of a hate crime.

Sean exhaled and made a dismissive comment that suggested I didn't know what I was talking about. We went to another commercial break, and that was the end of the interview. Sean's a pro, and once we were off the air, we did the customary salutations and he made no mention of my opinion about gay adoption.

I had a great time that week in New York. I also went down to Washington, D.C., for a day to do more interviews. I came to know another journalist, named Tony Snow, during that time and I was a guest on his radio show as well. Tony and I hit it off, and I feel lucky to have had a nice friendship with him in the years that followed. We saw each other on occasion, had lunch, attended the same events from time to time, but mostly we kept up with each other by e-mail.

I found Tony to be one of the more reasonable people in his field, and although we certainly did not agree on most things regarding politics, we did agree that there was a need for more civilized, informed discussions in the world. I received a note from Tony before he lost his fight with cancer. He said, "My friend, I'm listening to your CD today. Keep on keepin' on." I had a heavy heart the day Tony died.

A few weeks after my appearance on Sean Hannity's radio show, I was scheduled to head back to New York City to appear on the *Hannity & Colmes* television show on Fox News.

The show's taping was scheduled for evening, and I believe that my segment of singing and the brief interview was to be shown during the next night's program. I did a quick sound check, sang my song, and then was seated between Sean and Alan to do the sit-down interview. I'm not sure if Sean was pushing me or if I was pushing him, but we quickly came to a point at which we were "sparring" a bit. It was in good fun, I thought, but perhaps it wasn't the kind of banter that they'd hoped for. Maybe Sean relies on his country music friends to be well-behaved Republicans and to side with him on the issues.

My opinions on the few issues we did discuss that night put me more in line with the thinking of the left-leaning host, Alan Colmes. I did my best to inject humor into the situation. After all, I'm not a political analyst, a policymaker, or a professional in the field of politics. I wasn't combative or looking to be adversarial. I'm not certain what happened after I left the Fox News studios that night or the next day, but that segment never aired on the Fox News Network. Furthermore, I have never heard from Sean Hannity again. I don't wonder why.

Love Everybody

I met John Rich at Opryland in 1990. We performed in the *Country Music USA* show for several years together. Dean Sams, another cast member, started a band during that time, called Lonestar, and asked John to join his band. Lonestar and I would eventually land our first record contracts around the same time. After years of hit records and touring, the band made a change and replaced John. Lonestar's fame continued to rise and they celebrated even more success. John was trying new things and had hopes of having a career as a solo artist. He and I wrote a couple of songs together while he was trying to get his next record contract.

I headed out on the road for a year or so and didn't see or talk to John for a while, but when I did make it back to town, I caught up on the latest Music Row news. I learned that John and his pal Big Kenny had started a duo called Big and Rich. I thought that was clever and seemed to make sense. They really were friends and collaborators, and that type of situation usually works best for a band or duo dynamic. It has a better chance of being successful if it is authentic.

I also heard that John and Big Kenny had created a club made up of unique performers, mostly musicians, who were banding together to support one another's art. They were calling themselves the Muzik Mafia. Initially, they would gather at a club, play music, and hang out. The members were artists who'd been kicking around the Row for a while but for one reason or another hadn't had their big break.

They had a mantra: "Love Everybody." I liked the idea, in theory. John was the only one of the bunch that I knew. "Love Everybody"? I never bought into it, at least not from John. I believe the others in the club operated in the spirit of their mantra, but I knew John too well. John does not love everybody. It was always my opinion that John was exploiting certain people and capitalizing on the hopes and good intentions of others. The Muzik Mafia was all anyone talked about for a couple of years, and when asked about it, I was diplomatic in my response, if I commented at all. I was invited a couple of times to go to their parties, but it wasn't difficult for me not to show up; I could get away easily by blaming it on my schedule.

John and I made plans to get together one night in March 2005. We were both working near Music Row and when I finished my work, I headed over to Blackbird Studio, where he was working. I made small talk with a couple of the guys up front, then made my way back to the room where John and Big Kenny were mixing. They played a couple of tracks they were working on and I was excited by the music. One of the songs was called "Holy Water" and I thought it was a stand-out track.

John had just bought a new house ten minutes away and he asked me if I would go over and see it. I would never ask a friend to come to my house. Julia was there, and as a general rule we just didn't bring people into our home. I accepted John's invitation, and as we left Blackbird I headed to my car. Before I could get in it, John asked me to ride with him. I've always avoided riding with people. I never know what someone has had to drink, and I tend to feel kidnapped. I like to exit a place when I want to leave, not when someone gets around to giving me a ride. John asked me again to ride in his new Corvette that Chevrolet had given him. I'm not interested in cars, but John was proud of it. "All right," I said. "I'll ride in your 'look-at-me-I'm-a-star' car."

John drove too fast and too recklessly for my liking, but we arrived safely at his house. He showed me around with great excitement, and I loved seeing my old friend in a brand-new place. There is something cool about having started out with someone at the same time, being starving artists together, and then seeing each other enjoy success.

At John's home we watched basketball, drank cold beer, played guitars, and talked about our current and future projects. After the game, I told John it was time for me to head back to my car. He asked if I wanted to drive his car and I laughed and said no. We were back on the other side of town in just a few minutes and as we pulled into Blackbird's parking lot, John said, "Can I ask you a question?"

With great trepidation I said, "Yes."

"You know, people talk about you," he said. "They wonder if you're, you know, gay or something like that." He wasn't asking me a question, and I just sat there and tried not to show my panic. "You know, that's not cool, if you've chosen to live that kind of lifestyle. Fans won't have it. This industry won't allow it. This is country music. It's about God and country and family. People don't approve of that kind of deviant behavior. It's a sin."

He wasn't looking at me. He was fidgeting with buttons and knobs on the dashboard. I was staring out his windshield, looking at the back of my vehicle, wishing I were in it and driving away from this conversation. John seemed to be okay with my nonresponse and just kept on with his rant. I'd heard John say disparaging things about gays before, but now he was directing those words at me, and I was rattled.

He said he felt strongly that the speculation that I might be gay had damaged my career and that it was critical that I clear up the rumor. "I can help you. I'm in a great spot right now. Warner Brothers has basically written me a blank check to make any record I want, but I can't help you out if you don't take care of this crap."

I'd never implied that I needed or wanted John's help.

"The fans and radio love you," he said. "You could be a lot bigger than you are right now, but you gotta hit this gay thing head-on. You need to take out a press release or something and clear it up, let everybody know that you're not gay." I let out a nervous and defensive burst of air. He turned toward me in his driver's seat.

"You're not gay, are you?"

I took a deep breath and said, "No, John, I'm not gay."

"Good!" he said.

I told him that I needed to go. I got in my car and drove home. I was shaking and felt lightheaded. As I drove toward my house in West Nashville I was overcome with frustration and sadness. My situation was getting more and more difficult. Until that night I had never actually been put in a position that caused me to have to answer yes or no about my sexuality. Until that night I had never directly lied about it. I was ashamed of myself—not for being gay but for lying. I wondered just how complex my life would become, how much energy it was going to take to maneuver in my new level of dishonesty.

It took me a couple of days to tell Julia what had happened. She knew that I was bothered by something because I couldn't eat or sleep and I was agitated. She was concerned about how scary John was, but mostly she was concerned about how it was affecting me.

An added tragedy of the matter was that I knew that John was not alone in his disdain for gays when it came to the industry and fans of country music. John's rant played a part in validating my fears of being outed, and more than likely it influenced some of my decisions in the short term. Julia and I were having some trouble at that time. I was frustrated and hopeless about our chances of working it out or making it in the long term, and a week or so after my evening with John Rich, I began to look for a different house to live in. I had a crazy fantasy that even if Julia and I did make it, we would have to do it living separately.

The only person I told about that night was, of course, Julia. After I came out to my best friend, Chuck, a few months later, I told him about what John had said. We all agreed that it would be best to keep what we knew about John Rich's feelings toward homosexuals between us. As it turned out, it wouldn't be long before John himself would make his position on the topic a public issue.

John was a guest on a conservative radio talk show shortly after our "talk" in his car, and when asked about his stance on gay marriage he said: "I think if you legalize that [same-sex marriage], you've got to legalize some other things that are pretty unsavory. You can call me a radical, but how can you tell an aunt that she can't marry her nephew if they are really in love and sharing the bills? How can you tell them they can't get married, but something else that's unnatural can happen?"

There was such an uproar across the nation and on the Internet that John issued a statement to the press the very next day that said:

> My earlier comments on same-sex marriage don't reflect my full views on the broader issues regarding tolerance and the treatment of gays and lesbians in our society. I apologize for that and wish to state clearly my views. I oppose same-sex marriage because my father and minister brought me up to believe that marriage is an institution for the union of a man and a woman. However, I also believe that intolerance, big-

otry, and hatred are wrong. People should be judged based on their merits, not on their sexual orientation. We are all children of God and should be valued and respected.

Suffice it to say that, in my opinion, John Rich and the notion of equality and "Love Everybody" have never met.

Moving Out

When Julia and I broke up, it was a difficult and sad time for both of us. Although couples therapy had proven to be good for us, we were tired of fighting an unwinnable war.

Even after we broke up and moved out of our home, we continued to go sporadically to couples therapy. She finally admitted to me in therapy that for years whenever I'd have a record that struggled on the charts, she'd be overjoyed inside. She told me that she used to pray that my singles would fail and that MCA would drop me. I know it was humiliating for her to admit it after I'd been accusing her of exactly that for years. In her defense, she knew that as long as I did that job there would never be a place for her in the way she wanted and any kind of success might take me from her. Acknowledging each other as partners would have been a step toward being a healthier couple, but I couldn't risk it and we both knew it.

When you're gay you realize that, for the most part, a lot of the world hates you without having ever met you. It's unsettling. At times I was able to let that go, but it caused a tremendous strain on our feelings for one another.

I wanted to be able to be myself. I was one-half of a fully committed relationship and I had to hide that. Then I found myself, even in the privacy of my own home, having to omit certain parts of who I am. Like it or not, I was a well-known country music singer. I'd worked and dreamed my entire life to achieve that, and Julia simply did not like it. So, because I loved her, I left my work outside of our home. I wanted her, I wanted us to be together, and I did what I had to do to make it work. A part of me also felt like I didn't deserve to have it all. I don't believe that today.

Kristin

I never imagined that I might develop a relationship with someone else. But I did. I had gone to great lengths, by moving out of my home with Julia, to re-create my world and present myself as a straight single woman. The last thing I needed was to have a new person in my life. I'd just have to hide all over again. Nevertheless, I became involved with someone new. I wondered how long Julia and I would last, not being together. I was convinced that we just needed that time apart, to throw people off, and then we'd find a way to get back together.

I had a new record out and was doing the things asked of an artist by a record label—promotion and touring. Being out on the road at that time provided a nice distraction for me. I was numb from the breakup with Julia, but mostly I was consumed with the logistics of it all. We had to sell the house and we each had to buy a new house, all the while still living under the same roof. We'd been sleeping in different bedrooms for quite a while, but there was still a tension that lingered in the house until we finally went our separate ways.

I was working with a woman involved in the release of my current record at that time, and we soon became close. Several months into knowing one another, Kristin told me that she was attracted to me and that she couldn't stop thinking about me.

She confessed that she'd never been with a woman other than kissing her girlfriends when they were drunk. However, she said, she was cool with same-sex relationships—"chill" with it, to use her word. I was flattered but cautious.

At first she was fun and easy to be around, and that was refreshing to me. But there were moments early on where I saw things about her that I knew would be a challenge. One evening we went with a couple of other folks to the Nashville Sounds minor league baseball game. As we were walking out, a man was randomly handing out literature about Christianity. We each had the pamphlet in our hands as we talked about the game. "Isn't that ironic," she said, "that that man happened to randomly give all of us that literature—the four people at the stadium who don't believe in God?" She said that she wished she'd told the "Jesus freak" to buzz off.

"Kristin, I very much do believe in God," I objected. "I always have." I had told her I wasn't a member of a religious group or a church, but that didn't mean I was a non-believer. I didn't like the way she arrogantly scoffed at and belittled people who believed in God. Why would I even consider having a girlfriend who was not spiritual? My faith in God was part of me.

Kristin could be unpredictable and erratic. She would profess her love for me and then disappear for days at a time. She would say that she would be at my house by 6:30 p.m. to have dinner and not show up. Then she would text me three hours later and ask me what I was doing, as if nothing had happened. I understood the push and pull of being a closeted person in a gay relationship, but I sensed it was something more serious than that.

Kristin liked, as she put it, to get "hammered." She told me stories about her ex-boyfriend Bobby, who was a recreational drug user and a heavy drinker. She admitted that she drank heavily to cope with the sexual part of their relationship and she sometimes blacked out.

Kristin spent a lot of time getting drunk. The more she drank, the more she seemed to crave male attention. She was attractive and didn't have to work hard to get it. Often I'd end up babysitting her, trying to get her to eat something so she wouldn't vomit. I suspected Kristin's drinking problem was related to her problems dealing with her sexuality. I knew her drinking was dangerous for her, but one night I realized her drinking was dangerous for me.

Kristin and I flew to New York to spend time with my friends—a tradition, to meet in New York City and attend a holiday party. We arrived at the party, which was beautifully catered, with several bars and a dance floor in the tent area out back. Although Kristin was my girlfriend, we weren't out to anyone but Chuck, the only one of my friends who knew I was gay, so I mingled at the party as if I was there as a single person. I was used to doing that in public. At one point in the evening, I realized I didn't know where Kristin was and I asked my friends if they'd seen her. Someone said she was having one hell of a time.

Not a good sign.

I soon discovered Kristin gyrating on the dance floor by herself while a crowd of men watched. I stood by, drinking bottled water, and watched her invite two men to dance with her. By the third song, one man was on her front side and another behind her. She was straddling the leg of the man in front, while the man behind her was grinding his pelvis into her backside. She was laughing and yelling. I wasn't jealous; I was just mortified.

I finally caught her attention and asked her to sit down and have some food with me. She ate two pieces of shrimp before she stood up and said that she needed to use the restroom. She never came back. About half an hour later, I found her doing shots with more men neither of us knew.

Later, Chuck and I were talking when a friend approached us and grabbed each of us by the forearm. Her eyes were wide and frantic. "We've got a problem," she said. "Kristin's a lesbian and she's in love with Chely." In hushed tones, Anne Marie told us how Kristin, in her drunken state, had pulled her aside and told her.

Instead of discussing it further, the three of us searched the house for Kristin. We finally found her and pulled her into a bathroom. She was wasted. "Don't break up with me 'cause I got too drunk again," she kept saying. My friend's jaw dropped to the floor. There was no way to talk myself out of this situation. I told Anne Marie that I was gay and that Kristin was my girl-friend.

Anne Marie just hugged me and told me that she was sorry I was forced into telling her that way, but that she loved me and just wanted me to be happy. The party was winding down, so we headed back to Chuck's. When we got back, Kristin passed out. While she slept, I went downstairs to join the others and learned that she had spent much of the evening telling my friends about our relationship. I felt clammy and flushed. Chuck hugged me and said that everything was going to be okay.

Kristin's out-of-control behavior continued. I realized her fre-quent absences always seemed to coincide with meals. If I did get her to sit down to dinner, she'd pick at her food and say that she didn't feel well. When I questioned her about the behavior, she finally admitted that she purposely avoided eating so that she could get drunk more easily. She also revealed that she was bulimic; she starved herself during the day, then went home to binge. She had been making herself throw up for years. Kristin said that if we agreed early in the day to meet at 6:30 p.m. to go out to a restaurant, she would say yes but know from the start she wasn't going to show up. She also admitted that she often dropped plans we'd made if an offer to go out drinking came up. Drinking was the only thing that kept her mind off food. "I hate everything about who I am," she said. "Everything."

A few weeks later, I was on the road in California when Kristin called me from Nashville and announced that she had broken up with Bobby.

I had no idea what she was talking about. She had told me about her dark days with Bobby but had said she ended the relationship around the time we had gotten to know each other. But their relationship had continued, and she had decided to end it, leaving Bobby—who had had no idea about her relationship with me—devastated and confused. He began sending Kristin e-mails, begging her to give him another chance but also, at least initially, urging her not to fear her sexuality. Once I got over my shock, I read these e-mails and urged Kristin to at least respond to some of his questions about how she felt. After she had kept him in the dark for so long, it seemed to me, it was the least she could do.

Kristin ignored Bobby's pleas. I feared that further angering Bobby would provoke some kind of action against her—and me. And it did. Soon he was sending e-mails to others about Kristin's relationship with me. These anonymous e-mails began finding their way to Kristin's boss, then to country star Ricky Skaggs, then to her mother and father and to two journalists at the *Nashville Tennessean* (who, fortunately, were personal friends of Kristin's so they kept the information to themselves). The message was clear—Bobby wasn't going to be ignored, even if it meant exposing me to avoid it.

Bobby sent me some of Kristin's early e-mails from before she cut off all communication with him. In them she told him that I had been flirting with her and that she had been ashamed of the idea of being gay or bisexual. She told him she was curious enough to try to take things further with me, but that nothing long-term would ever come of it because the thought of being gay disgusted her. She did not tell him that she had initiated our relationship.

Although I had by this time revealed my sexuality to a small circle of trusted people, I had continued to carefully guard my secret. It had been a risk to let Kristin in. But when her feud with Bobby engulfed me, I begged her to confront him. "You need to reach out to him and stop this," I told her. "You need to fix this situation. Please, be a grown-up and clean up your mess." But she did nothing.

Still, I didn't walk away from Kristin. I cared for her, despite all the headaches she was causing me. I knew too well what she was going through, and I wanted to support her. I was really unhealthy myself, though. I was trying so hard to save her rather than focus on making my own life healthier. I knew that the only way I could be healthy was to stop hiding and running from the fact that I was gay. But saving myself, in those terms, was not an option. So I continued to try to save her. I convinced myself that I had chosen Kristin over Julia (perhaps I had) and if I let the relationship between Kristin and me fail, it would prove that I had made a mistake in leaving Julia. I was bound and determined to make it work, and it didn't have much to do with Kristin. I was a closeted woman. If I broke it off with Kristin, I'd have no chance of having partnership and love. It's difficult to find people to date while you're in the closet. I took what I could and tried to make the best of it.

Even though we lived around the corner from each other, the only way Kristin could truly speak freely was by calling me on the telephone. Despite her reckless behavior that outed me to my friends, she was worried about her friends and neighbors discovering our relationship. She rarely invited me to her home, and if she did, she asked me to park my car far enough away not to arouse suspicion. When I complied, it made me feel full of shame. The progress I had made in coming to terms with my own identity over the years had been significant, but I didn't stay away from Kristin, destructive as the situation was to my well-being.

Fear was overtaking me again. I was seeing just how big a bombshell my secret was. I'd never doubted my reasons for hiding, but now I knew for sure I wasn't just being paranoid. Having someone package up my secret and anonymously mail it to others in my industry in an effort to destroy my reputation and my career validated my hiding all those years. The anonymous mailer wasn't spilling the beans that I was a little bit pigeon-toed or that I got two speeding tickets in one week back in 1991. No—he knew that my being gay, if revealed, could hurt me in profound ways. The realization that Kristin had recklessly given Bobby the ammunition to exact his malice on me was terrifying. My continuing to see her made it worse.

My Dad

I decided in the fall of 2005 that it was time to come out to my dad. I didn't want to, but I needed to. Hiding causes all kinds of problems. When someone doesn't have all of the information, or at least a fair and reasonable amount of it, problems pop up. That had been happening with my dad and me.

I had made a habit of not answering my phone, especially when the person who was calling was someone who didn't know my secret. Every time my dad would dial my phone I'd let it go to voice mail and then call him back when I was ready. It was too difficult to make up a lie or omit the truth so frequently.

For more than a decade I'd spent all of my free time and most of my holiday time with Julia, and I got tired of making up little lies about what I was doing when a phone call came in. So I'd wait until a weekday, when she would be at work, and then I'd return calls. The trouble with my policy was that my dad was busiest during the week, and when I would call him back he was unable to talk. Months would go by without actually having any kind of real conversation, and it was driving a wedge between us.

One day I was at my house when I returned a call to my dad. It was a weekday during work hours, and I hoped to be able to just leave a voice mail on his cell phone. Instead, he picked up. "Hey, kid! Where the heck have you been?" he asked, in a light and playful tone. I was used to his making remarks that the father of a grown and busy woman might make, the usual repeated requests to call him or come see him more often. "I know, I know, Pippy. I'm just always so busy. I'm sorry," saying what I always said. That's when he said that he wanted to talk to me about something. I got a sick feeling in my stomach and I said, "Okay, what's going on?"

He said that he was very confused about why we hadn't been close the way we used to be, that it really hurt his feelings and that he wanted to have a better relationship with me. He asked if there was anything that he'd done wrong; was I angry with him? He said he was sorry for whatever he'd done. He said that his second wife, Verna, whom I love and like, had encouraged him to just ask me why we didn't have a closer relationship.

I told him that he'd done nothing wrong and that I wanted to have a closer relationship with him too. I explained it away as best I could to make him believe me, going on and on about how busy I was and how I didn't have time to talk to anyone. I promised I would try to do a better job of making time for him. He seemed to be appeased with my reasons and excuses, and I felt momentarily relieved. I knew that I'd done nothing more than put a Band-Aid on a gaping flesh wound.

During the next few days and weeks, I felt a tugging at my conscience and wondered how long I was going to do this to my dad. I'd come out to my sister, Jeny, a year before that, in September of 2004, and it had proven to be a good thing in my life. But coming out to Jeny and coming out to my father were two different things.

In basic terms, my dad is a country boy—raised on the farm in rural Missouri, dropped out of school in the eighth grade, joined the navy as soon as he could.

I'd always been afraid that he would not understand my being gay. There had been jokes and stories told at the dinner table my entire childhood that were derogatory toward gays. I didn't feel safe enough to confide in anyone in my family or in my life for so long, and my father was no exception.

When I was a little girl, I loved having my dad's approval. Now that I was a grown woman, his endorsement was still important to me. I'd always made him proud and I knew it.

My folks had had so much fun helping me with my career. When I moved to Nashville and was on my own and making it happen on a much bigger scale, their pride grew exponentially. There wasn't a soul back home who didn't know that Stan and Cheri's little girl had made it big. How could I ever ruin that for him? I guess part of it too was that I wanted to protect him from an uncomfortable, embarrassing situation. I would often wonder what it would be like for my dad if his friends or his coworkers found out that I was gay. They'd always been excited about my fame and successes, and they'd all put my picture or my calendar up in their shops and barns. What would that be like for my dad? Would he be ashamed of me?

I suppose that way down in my heart I thought he would. So I did what a lot of gay people choose to do—I decided to spare him. It wasn't fair of me, but that's what I did.

Weeks went by and I stopped being consumed with worry about the conversation with my dad. I simply made a commitment to myself to do a better job of calling him.

Not long after we'd had our phone conversation, Kristin's ex-boyfriend, Bobby, had restarted his e-mail campaign of terror, and this time he seemed to be gunning only for me. I was not going to have Bobby be the one to determine how and when my dad would learn about me.

I was headed back to Missouri to do a show in a little town called El Dorado Springs, which happened to be my dad's boy-hood hometown, and I decided to come out to my father. Dad called to tell me he would be at the show. I told him that I'd love to see him.

The night before we pulled into El Dorado, I didn't sleep well on the bus. I was scared and I wondered if I'd have the nerve to go through with it. I got up early, had my oatmeal, and went for a long walk. When I got back to my room, I sat nervously. I didn't make phone calls and I didn't turn on the TV to distract myself. It seemed like the longest afternoon of my life. There was a small General Electric clock radio on the nightstand next to the bed, and the little red digital numbers seemed to struggle too.

My father arrived at my hotel room at around three o'clock, typically the best time for us to visit when I was on the road. It amused him to watch me transform myself during the hair and makeup process.

Dad knocked on my hotel room door and I let him in. "Hey, my little Pippy!" I said with a shaky voice. I didn't see Verna with him, and he told me that he'd decided to come by himself because there was going to be a lot of be-boppin' around backstage and out in the crowd too, since this was his old stomping ground. I could tell he was excited about the evening to come. He gave me a hug, though, sent from Verna.

I began to tremble before the door to the room closed behind us. I think I offered him a bottle of water. He asked me in that playful voice of his, "So what's been going on, kiddo?" I didn't hesitate—I didn't make small talk at all. I said, "Dad, I need to talk to you. I need to tell you something." In what looked like slow motion, he bent his knees and without even looking to see where he was going to sit, he sat. I sat next to him on the edge of the bed.

He was turned toward me at about forty-five degrees, and I was turned toward him at the same angle. I had planned so carefully what I was going to say. I'd practiced such an elegant, calm, informative, and confident speech in the days that led up to that moment. But instead, my face just contorted and I began to cry. I began to do the kind of crying where you can't speak. He had a really frightened look on his face, but his fatherly instincts kicked in and he hugged me and held on to me. He was patting my back and the back of my head. He said, without pausing for me to answer his rapid-fire questions, "It's okay. You're okay. Are you? Are you okay? You're not okay? What's wrong? Are you sick? Do you have cancer? If you're sick, we'll be okay. We'll get through it."

Even if he had let me answer, I couldn't have. I pulled back from him, just enough to see his face, and he was crying too. He had never, in the thirty-five years of my life, seen me so unable to gain my composure. I looked him in the eye and knew that it could very well be the last time those eyes of his would see me this way. I stared down at my hands and slowly dismantled an already soaked Kleenex. I stuttered and stammered. I'd never had a problem putting words together from the stage or in a conversation to articulate my thoughts and feelings, until that moment.

"Dad, there's something that I need to tell you. It's something that I've needed to tell you my whole life and I haven't done it because I'm scared. I'm scared that you'll be disappointed in me or you'll be mad at me or you won't want to call me your daughter anymore. It's something that I've known my whole life, and hiding it has caused me incredible pain for a long, long time." With a great pause and noticeable hesitance, he said, "Okay." I took a deep breath and blew it out like a weight lifter does when pushing a three-hundred-pound barbell away from his chest. "Dad, I'm gay." I looked up at his eyes. He said, "You are?" To which I replied, "Mmm-hmmm." He said flatly, "Okay."

I wondered then, and still wonder, what was going through his head at that moment. He was confused, and that didn't surprise me at all. I was prepared to answer whatever questions he might have for me. He asked me, "What about those boys you dated—what about them?" I explained to him that I tried so hard to love them the way that they loved me, but I just couldn't.

I told him that they didn't know that I was gay and that I'd hurt some of them pretty badly and I felt horrible about it. I also told him that I'd prayed to God since I was a little girl to change me, to make me normal, and that no matter what I did I was still gay. I shared with him the struggle I've had in my professional life to keep my secret.

Right when I felt like he was understanding what I was saying, he'd ask a question or make a comment that made me realize that it was going to take more than two hours to explain it all. "But, Chel, you're so pretty. You could date most any guy you wanted." "But, Squirrelly, are you sure? You like wearing dresses and stuff. You really don't look like that kind of person—you know, a gay person." I nodded and said that I understood his thoughts but I was certain that I was gay.

Then, after the initial shock, he got a little angry with me for keeping it from him. He said I'd cheated him out of knowing me and being closer to me. "Why on God's green earth would you not tell me this until now?" he asked. I didn't want to answer. He pressed on. "Why?" It broke my heart to do it, but I reminded him of all of the jokes about gays and the poking fun at gays that I'd heard from him and my entire family, not to mention from everyone in my little town of Wellsville, Kansas.

He buried his face in his hands and sobbed. "I'm sorry, I'm sorry, I'm sorry—I'm so sorry."

Now I was the one consoling him. "You didn't know, Dad. It's okay. I'm not mad at you about it. I know you didn't know." He hugged me really hard. I became a little girl again, wanting and needing his approval. "Do you still love me, even though?" I asked. He grabbed me by the shoulders, looked me square in the eye, and said, "Honey, I don't still love you even though—I love you because."

He went on to tell me some things that I have always felt from him but had never heard him say. He actually said that I was and had always been one of the best friends he'd ever had in his life and that he had always admired me for so many reasons. He told me that he didn't adore me just because I'd gone on to reach my dreams in country music. He said that all of that was pretty neat, but the reason he adored me so much was because of the person I am—kind, compassionate, and just good.

When I imagined coming out to my dad, I didn't envision that there would be a portion of the conversation like this. He said that he wasn't quite sure that he understood it all, and I told him that was okay.

He took his ball cap off his head with his right hand, and with that same hand scratched his hair and rubbed his forehead. Then he said to me, "All I know is this, kiddo—if you try to be something in this life that you're not, you won't be very goddamn good at it." He pulled his cap back down on his head. "You know it?" "Yes, I know it," I said.

He left the room, headed out to find the bus and the guys in the band. I took another shower to cool my flushed skin and to get my body temperature down to a normal range, then I got into hair and makeup. I felt weak and strong all at the same time. I was relieved, but I was nervous about how my dad would digest the news over the next few hours.

That night we had a great show there in the city square of my dad's hometown. There were several thousand people in attendance, and my dad was the real star. I called him up onstage and the crowd went crazy. He grabbed the mic from me and told the audience how proud he was that Chely Wright was his daughter. No one knew, in that crowd or on that stage, what he was saying, what his words meant—but I did.

I knew what he was saying.

He thanked everyone for being at the show, and then he gave me a strict order right into the microphone: "Get back to work and sing for these people!"

The Boy Scouts of America

In the summer of 2005 the band, the crew, and I headed to Dallas, Texas, for a private show.

During my years at Opryland, I learned the ins and outs of doing private shows for companies like AT&T, Saturn, Ford Motor Company, Kimberly-Clark, and others. These shows are typically part of a once-a-year celebration or convention for a company or organization. I enjoyed the challenge of making their events memorable, and I take pride in customizing the show just for them.

After the band and crew had the gear and the stage set up, my tour manager, Jan Volz, came to my hotel room to escort me down to sound check. As we were walking to the venue, he told me that the show was for the Boy Scouts of America. That night was to be the final night of a three-day conference. The people in the audience were the most prominent people involved with the Boy Scouts of America, and many of them had made significant financial contributions over the years and had traveled from all over the country to attend the special event. Jan made arrangements for me to speak to the person in charge of the entertainment for the evening so I would know who was sitting in front of me and so I could get a feel for the event.

Jan located the man in charge, and the three of us stepped outside the ballroom to talk. He was a charming man in his early sixties, and he told me that the planning committee was excited about my performing for them. They liked my music and, more important, they liked what I stood for. I wondered what it was they thought I stood for.

The organizer quickly added that the Boy Scouts of America knew that I must be one of them because of the support that I'd shown for the troops and the many times that I'd traveled overseas to perform for them.

I asked him questions that I thought would help me best entertain the audience. Toward the end of my list of questions, he told me to have fun with the crowd but emphasized that I needed to be careful not to say anything that would be offensive.

Jan and I looked at one another. The gentleman continued to talk. He told us that the Boy Scouts of America had been in the media quite a bit in the past few years and it wouldn't be appropriate if I were to make a joke about the lawsuits and the media coverage, as it was still a sensitive topic to the organization. I nodded my head, listening. He laughed a deep belly laugh and said, "We're a strong group with a strong set of history and morals. We don't allow women and we don't allow the gays."

A rush of blood went to my head. Even though Jan didn't know my secret at the time, he shared my reaction to what had just been said. Jan and I didn't make eye contact until we got into the elevator. We looked at each other, jaws dropped, and shook our heads from side to side in disbelief about what had just happened.

I had a couple of hours before the performance, which was unfortunate, because it allowed me time to get all wound up about it. I considered refusing to do the show.

I called my sister and told her what had happened, and when I told her that I was not going to do the show, she asked me what my excuse for canceling would be. Would I be willing to admit that I wouldn't play for them because of their exclusion of women and gays? And if I did, wasn't I afraid that that would draw attention to my sexuality? She was right. Not to mention that if I canceled, I would have been in breach of contract, and I would have incurred a huge expense for flights, hotel rooms, and employees who would still be expected to be paid for their time whether they played the show or not. I decided that I should do the show and take the money that I was paid by the Boy Scouts of America.

As I performed that night, I was agitated. I purposely failed to say a special thanks to the committee and the gentleman in charge of entertainment, as I usually do at a private show. During the show, I got an idea about how I might be able to feel better about having gone ahead with the performance.

Once I was back in Nashville, I had my business manager give me a spreadsheet showing the amount of profit I made on the job. I went to the bank and got a money order in that exact amount. I mailed it anonymously to a nonprofit organization that assists gays and lesbians with outreach programs in the state of Tennessee. Although I did feel some slight relief in having done that, I still felt shame. I felt like a coward for not fighting for what I really stood for; instead I made a gesture that went largely unnoticed.

Now I have the courage to make my voice known to everyone, not just to me.

Run, Jeny, Run

There are two kinds of hot in the Midwest—dry hot and sticky hot. One particular summer was about to offer both. I was ten years old. It was late in the month of May 1981, and just like all the years before it, we'd ended the school year in Kansas with unseasonably high temperatures.

The year before, my parents' *git'er done* mantra once again spilled over onto the three of us kids, and our family of five found ourselves building a house on a tiny piece of land that a benevolent local farmer named Clarence Moldenhauer had given my parents on a handshake that they'd somehow, someday pay him back, which they eventually did. My folks had bought a used modular home, which was no more than a double-wide trailer, but before it was delivered, my dad brought in some heavy equipment and had an enormous hole dug in the ground. We put up steel panels and lots of wood to create forms into which concrete would be poured, and that gray, sticky mud would eventually become a basement and the foundation for our home.

I recall that my sister and I had a specific job for several days that seemed never to end. Our task: each would carry a five-gallon bucket full of gravel back and forth about fifty yards up a hill, take it to the edge of the drop-off at the new foundation, and dump it between the outside wall of the concrete and the earth. In construction terms, it's called backfilling—and it's backbreaking. The combination of dust from the ground and chalk dust from the rock made it difficult to breathe, and every time I tipped my bucket over into the big gap below, it shocked me as to how much of a difference the new gravel *didn't* make.

Jeny was strong, and whenever my dad needed help lifting, pulling, or pushing—though obviously he could count on my brother—we all knew that my sister possessed the real brawn. Without anyone else's help, she and my dad lifted and set the I-beams into place on that basement, and a day later our home would be lowered onto those beams. Once that phase of the project was complete, we moved on. We dug our own water lines and sewer lines and installed a cistern and a septic tank. At last, we were in the house we called home.

That first summer, while working hard, we had our fun too. We'd come to love the huge pond on Clarence's property that sat just behind our house; it was clear and deep, and it did all the things a good Kansas pond should do. It watered the horses that roamed the surrounding fields, and it gave a home to the sun-perch, the bass, and whatever the heck that big thing was that bumped into my leg twice while we were night swimming. The pond was our playground, and nearly every hot day we'd take a dip. Sometimes it was just a matter of getting our bodies cooled off, because we didn't have air-conditioning in our house. (We did finally get central air my senior year of high school.)

I remember one of the first days we got to enjoy the pond was the day after my mom had showed Jeny and me how to float on our backs. Chris was at the pond, too, but he was on the shore with Darren—Clarence's grandson, who was just a year older than my brother and always around; they were trying to repair a dilapidated, homemade diving board made of 2x6's.

Jeny and I were floating side by side on our backs in the middle of the twenty-seven-foot-deep pond, and I was relaxed and perfectly buoyed. There was no wind that day and the surface looked like glass. My legs dangled in the abyss below (even though it freaked me out a little bit that that thing was down there), my ears were submerged, and the water line was just at my cheekbones. Jeny wouldn't hold still, and her movement was annoying me because it was causing the water to wave and lap up over my face, into my nose and mouth.

"Stop moving!" I said, like a ventriloquist, so I didn't cause more ripples myself.

I opened my eyes to see if I could determine why she kept lifting her head up and out of the water. I caught her. She'd been stealing glances at Darren over by the dock.

After that day, I started to notice other signs, and I could tell that Jeny had it bad for Darren. It was the first crush I ever knew her to have, and I don't even think she told me she had it. At that time Jeny was eleven, I was nine, and although we had a normal sister relationship, she didn't confide in me that she thought Darren was a stone-cold fox. Which he kind of was. He wore T-shirts with the sleeves ripped off, and he had crazy unkempt curly hair bleached by the sun, tanned skin, and a big smile. He was the apple of his grandfather's eye, and everybody called him "Wild Man." For such a young kid, Darren was responsible and a great help to his grandpa in handling the duties of the farm, which were many. But as hard as he worked, he played. Darren tooled around on tractors, in trucks, and on a red three-wheeler with huge tires that allowed him to drive it right into the pond and straight to the other side.

If you were a young girl of eleven, and you were my sister, you were looking for a boy like Darren.

So for our second summer in the country, there was no construction project and in a way, it was our first *real* summer vacation there. I had survived the stresses of my fourth-grade year, and because of the added anxiety of feeling like an alien, I needed a break. More and more, Chris had been helping Clarence and Darren with farm chores, and his summer, much to his excitement, would be dedicated to working and getting paid.

Perhaps Jeny had to talk herself into being excited about the thought of a three-month summer break. Although she got picked on at school for being overweight, she didn't get much of an escape from the ridicule when she was home. The difference was, at school if someone called her a name, she could tell them to "shove it." She definitely could not do that at home.

For years, my mom and dad had been hard on Jeny about being heavy, and in the months that led up to that summer, their fervor was ratcheting up. They called her names like "Jeny Pig" and "Tush Hog," even encouraging and instructing my brother and me to call her by her newly given names. Instead of taking the time to seek out something special for her to wear that might make her feel more confident about her body, my mother made Jeny wear Husky brand jeans from the boys' department at Sears, saying, "If she gets embarrassed enough, she'll stop eating like a pig." I remember thinking how weird it was for my dad to call Jeny fat, when we all saw him struggle with diets every day and knew that he had been overweight as a child.

On the first day of our summer vacation, Jeny and I slept in as late as possible, but when we did arise, we had excitement rushing through our veins. There was so much to explore and so much to do. First, we did our chores. We mowed grass, put laundry on the line, then swept out the garage. The very garage, I'm convinced, that had an industrial dirt factory located beneath its concrete slab floor, and all of the workers below got a real kick out of the Wright kids as we tried to eliminate the filth.

As soon as we were set free, we headed up to a small barn that sat atop a hill on our property. The lower two-thirds was filled with chickens and spools of barbed wire, and in a couple of years it would house my beloved western saddle along with my other horse tack. The top of that barn had a shallow loft, and that was our first destination of the afternoon. Jeny and I scaled the ladder leading up to the hideaway, and we nested ourselves alongside a couple of Banty hens who were less than impressed with our drop-in visit. There was a fresh layer of straw in the loft, and it poked at our legs as we sat, Indian-style, in our shorts. It was hotter than you know what in that loft. There wasn't a shade tree around, and the tin roof over us was being punished by the three o'clock sun.

Our plan was to sit up there, get hot and sweaty, then run like maniacs across the pasture and jump headfirst into the pond. I'm guessing it was at least 110 degrees up there, so it didn't take long before we were drenched. We climbed down and raced for the water. It was as big a shock as we'd hoped it would be, going from that extreme hot to a cool country pond. We got acclimated to the temperature and then played the water games we always played; some we even made up on our own. Handstands; Who can hold their breath underwater the longest? (impossible for sisters to judge when no one's wearing a watch); Dive to the bottom of the pond's deepest part and bring up mud to prove you went all the way down; Can you see how many fingers I'm holding up underwater? Those were our games.

After a couple of hours, we decided it was time to go home. We crawled up onto the one shore that was pebbles rather than mud and put our still-a-little-wet tennis shoes on our feet. We headed back to the house, only a hundred and fifty yards away, strolling along the pond dam that towered above our backyard. Just as we made it to the top of the dam and got a glimpse of our mom and dad in the backyard, I guess they got their glimpse of us too.

"Jennifer!" they both shouted. "Get down here!"

Jeny froze. She looked at me and I gave her my best "What did you do?" look. They both yelled again, similar versions of "Get your ass down here now!"

She hurried down the incline of the dam, opened the gate that kept the horses from getting out, and latched the gate behind her. Although I was not in a hurry to walk in the direction of whatever it was that was happening, I did start to slowly make my way down. It was the only way to get to the house, which I desperately wanted to do. I was afraid I was next.

They were clearly angry with her, and even though people's homes weren't in close proximity out there in the country, I'm sure every neighbor could hear my parents screaming and cursing at my then twelve-year-old sister.

"If you won't do it, we'll do it for you."

"We won't have it, Jennifer, you better believe that!"

She was standing close enough to them to be hit, should one of them take a swipe at her, so she stood with both hands up high in front of her chest in preparation for what might come. She was not crying, but she looked scared, confused, and profoundly hurt. My brother wasn't home, and I kept hoping that he or someone would come to the rescue.

They were behind my mom's car, and they said, "Put it on." "Go ahead, Jeny Pig, put it on."

My dad handed her one end of a long, leather dog leash and told her to put it around her waist. The other end was tied to the bumper of the car. Jeny stared at them and didn't move. There was strength in her stillness, and I hoped that my folks were smart enough or kind enough to see it this time and back off. Unfortunately, they were not and they did not.

My mom said to my dad, "Get the strap."

My dad had a razor strap (a wide, thin strip of leather) in his shop that he kept for sharpening knives and lawn mower blades, but as helpful as that leather was for keeping implements in top form, it was more commonly used in our house as a tool for keeping kids in line.

My dad had the strap, and I was praying that Jeny would take off before he could get her, but she didn't. He smacked her hard across the back of her thighs. My mom got in the car, started the engine, and revved it up.

"Now put it on!" they screamed over six cylinders.

Jeny put the leash around her waist and fastened the brass

hardware like she was told to do. I remember seeing the leash around her center and how it cinched her in the middle of that white tank top with the little blue anchors on it. Now she *was* crying, and her face was as red as her cotton gym shorts, still soaked with pond water.

"We will not have a fat kid!"

"You're gonna run if we have to drag you."

My dad gave Jeny a couple more warning wallops on her legs to ensure that she was going to go along with her new workout regimen.

And so on the first day of summer vacation, my mom drove her Mercury Monarch out of our driveway, down the country road to the railroad tracks and back, with her oldest daughter, Jennifer, tied to the bumper of the car with a dog leash.

I was scared Jeny wouldn't be able to keep up and that she'd trip and fall down, but I was also afraid that Darren, the boy she'd quietly liked for the past year, would be driving that same country road at just the wrong time and see her like that.

I felt thankful that it wasn't me and also guilty that it wasn't. Events like this didn't occur with great frequency (about once a year), but knowing that something bad was coming and not knowing when it would arrive was nerve-racking.

The worst of what was happening to Jeny was not being whipped with a strap or dragged with a rope but rather the slow attempted murder of her spirit.

Down on My Knees

When my thoughts would become too scary or dark, a beautiful image would appear as a counterattack. The images didn't linger. They were stealthy—as suddenly as they appeared, they faded away.

I realized that I wasn't going to be able to take my own life. Not only was I scared to do it, but there was some part of me urging me to fight. I knew the old me, the strong me, was somewhere, trying to get through.

I found it difficult to make it through even an hour without breaking down, though. I was exhausted from crying and I was exhausted from trying not to cry. When I finally got out of bed, days after holding a gun in my mouth, I didn't make it much farther than the carpeted floor by my bed. I'd been saying prayers to God since the day it all began, but on this day my approach to prayer was different. I actually knelt by my bed, put my elbows up on the edge of the mattress, clasped my hands together, and rested my forehead on my hands. I prayed a different kind of prayer. I began to speak to God out loud. As I forced words to come out of my mouth, I realized that my voice was scratchy and weak. I knew God would hear me even if I didn't speak the words, but I wanted God to know that I was committed to my plea.

I did not pray that Kristin would call or that she and I would work it out. I didn't ask Him to stop the crying or the pain for good. I simply asked for a moment's peace. I asked God to please grant me a second or a minute or whatever amount of time He saw fit of peace. "Peace." I'd heard that word used my entire life in so many contexts—war and peace, a peaceful meadow, peace be with you—but I never really knew what it meant until that moment.

In God's name, I prayed. Still on my knees, with fingers interwoven, I sat back on my heels and exhaled.

I felt relief. I didn't have to think about it or analyze whether or not I was getting the peace that I had asked for; there was no confusion. I experienced a complete sense of peace from the inside out and realized that I'd just been given a gift. I cried, but not one tear was shed from despair. The tears came from gratitude. When I spoke two more words aloud, I noticed that the gravel in my voice was gone and it took almost no effort to project those words. The sound of the words was even musical; like two different notes, I said, "Thank you."

I had to do something because "Thank you" was not enough. I wanted to do something different to show God that I knew I'd just been given a massive dose of grace and mercy. I should not, I could not, I would not squander this gift, I thought.

I got up off my bedroom floor and went down to the second floor of the house. I made a stop in the laundry room and put two sweatshirts on top of the long-underwear thermal top and long-sleeved shirt that I was already wearing. I had a pair of flannel pajama bottoms on and a pair of long-underwear thermal bottoms underneath those. Then I made my way down to the first floor, kicked off my slippers, and put on my tennis shoes over the two pair of stretched-out socks that I'd had on for days.

I keep a tube of lip balm in the entryway of the house, and before I headed out the door, I reached for it. It sat on the mantel and as I grabbed it, I noticed the gun. I took the lid off of the Burt's Bees Lip Balm and smeared it on my lips, all the while staring at the gun. It looked different to me in the daylight. Smaller, less significant, almost like a toy. I did not touch it. I stepped out onto the front porch of my East Nashville house and noticed that the sky was spitting a little snow.

My plan had been to bundle up and go for a walk. A little snow wouldn't hurt me. I glanced to my left and saw my old bicycle sitting there on the porch. It was an inexpensive bike that I'd bought years ago at Target for $79. A few miles from my house was Shelby Park, which had a beautiful paved greenway that ran along the Cumberland River, but I hadn't ridden since the fall. I pushed on the tires of my bike and was surprised that they still had air in them. I figured I couldn't ride the three miles to the park, but I could at least go around the block a few times. I was skinny, tired, and weak, but I got on. Some people build a statue as a monument to mark a significant occasion or event. Some people write a song and dedicate it to the one they want to honor. Braving the cold on my bike would be my gesture to let God know that I was thankful for my moment of peace.

After the first few blocks, I felt a burn in my chest. The air was so cold that it stung every inch of tissue it touched, starting on the inside of my nose, to the back of my throat, through my windpipe, then finally exploding in the center of my lungs. It hurt, but it was a good hurt. The muscles in my legs were quivering, not because of the cold but due to lack of use—I'd been bed-bound for a month.

I remember every revolution of my pedals from that ride. I thought of nothing but being on that bike, and that my only duty in life left me focused on turning those wheels.

As it turned out, I didn't ride around the block. I rode to that park, over the entire eight miles of greenway, and back home. I rode thirteen miles in flannel pajama bottoms in the snow. I was building a statue—a monument of thanks, paying honor to God

My beloved Scott CR1 Road Bike. After I took that ride in the snow in my pajamas on my old bike, I continued to ride nearly every day. I rode alone for a long time—nearly a year. Then my rides slowly became something I shared with others. Now it's all about happiness, fun, health, and friends. 2008. (Jan Volz)

for the gift He'd just given me. "Keep pedaling, keep pushing, keep fighting for a breath," I said to myself. "Because you are thankful."

I got home, took a hot bath, and put on a fresh set of pajamas. I heated up a can of tomato soup in the microwave and forced it down. As I headed up to the third floor for the evening, I picked up the gun, carried it upstairs, and put it back where I'd found it a few days before.

Keep Your Friends Close, and Your Enemies Closer

I have been thinking a lot lately about people in my life. The reality is that I let many of them stay or treat me poorly because I was afraid of them.

I'd confided in a couple of people that I was gay, but there were other people in my life whom I hadn't told, though they were close to me and knew many specific details about me. Perhaps their knowledge of my life led them to make assumptions. I couldn't control what they thought they'd figured out. I certainly could have made the choice not to have friends, but that's not how I wanted to live.

I wanted friendships in my life, and if some of those people knew that I shared a house with a woman and that we spent our holidays and vacations together, that was just how it had to be. Now, as I recall those years, I realize that I allowed myself to be held hostage by a couple of those relationships.

I had an employee for a few years with whom I'd had a business relationship since the mid-1990s. She'd been close enough to me since that time to know certain personal details of my life, but I didn't confide in her that I was gay until late 2005. My doing so was really a matter of necessity; otherwise, I would have left it as it had been for a decade.

I'd wanted to end our working relationship for a couple of

years because I needed someone with more experience in her position. Before she worked for me, she worked for a large corporation, and I knew that she used the company credit cards for personal expenses, often taking her friends and family out for meals. After she began working for me, there were times that I thought the expense reports she turned in were questionable. I suspected that I (my corporation) was buying meals here and there for her and maybe for her family too. I wanted to tell her that whether or not what she was doing was technically stealing or illegal, it was sneaky and unethical. I didn't because I was afraid that she'd use my secret against me. I felt trapped.

There was an incident one summer where she went too far. She was adept at keeping certain things from me when dealing with my business associates. There is a particular advantage to being selective about the truth, and she put together a scenario that I wouldn't have endorsed and she knew it. I suspect she thought that I'd never delve into all of the details of it, but I did. This time, though, the one who was slighted in funds was not my company or her former company—it was a nonprofit organization with which I work on occasion.

I carefully gathered the facts, then had a meeting with her and asked her to explain it to me. I laid out the information I had and gave her a chance to correct me if I was wrong. She claimed she'd just been kidding with the nonprofit when she told them they'd have to satisfy certain needs of hers in order for the tour to happen. They met her needs, however, and she was fully aware of it every step of the way. She hadn't been kidding with them—she just didn't think that I'd find out.

Thousands of dollars were spent on satisfying her "needs," which she was allegedly joking about. She would even go on to accept cash from the organization. If she'd been sneaky with my business, I would be the one to lose. I allowed that because I was afraid to have her hurt me, but I wasn't going to allow a charity to be forced to spend more than it needed to.

Days after our meeting, she e-mailed me and said she thought she had explained what had happened and asked me why I couldn't just let it go. She claimed that the organization wouldn't even notice the financial hit—a weak rationalization. I told her I'd made up my mind: she had been unethical.

A few days later, she e-mailed and said that she was resigning.

I knew that by confronting her I'd made myself vulnerable, and I worried about whom she would gossip to.

Another person who was close to me for a long time—and is no longer in my life—started out as an intern in an office that handled my career. I eventually hired Brandon to work exclusively for me. After a few years, he moved on to another position with a new company and I was happy for him. We remained good friends, and he became friends with the other people who were close to me. We spent holidays together, leaned on each other during hard times, and shared in each other's lives.

Although Brandon was no longer my employee, he was still involved in some of my work-related functions like Reading, Writing & Rhythm, a nonprofit organization that I founded. Brandon's involvement was an integral part of its success.

Brandon would make up fantastic stories—some might call them lies. All of our friends would laugh at his tales, and on occasion we'd ask one another if a particular story was true. They rarely were—he wasn't careful about keeping his details straight, telling each of us slightly different versions. The few instances when we all took the time to compare details left us laughing. "That's just Brandon," we would say.

His reaction to being challenged was to be nasty and mean. This often happened when he was intoxicated. His inhibitions would be down and his retaliatory impulses up. He had a sharp tongue, and it was never good to be on the receiving end of one of his rants, but he seldom attacked me.

During my breakdown in early 2006, when I needed my friends the most, Brandon and I came to a juncture in our long relationship. I was on the phone with a mutual friend who asked me if I'd talked to Brandon in the past few days, and if so, did I know how he was feeling. The friend told me that Brandon had been having episodes of blacking out and that he had been told by his doctors that he had some kind of lesion or growth on his brain.

I quickly sent Brandon an e-mail asking him how he was doing. Later that evening, I was shopping in a boutique, near downtown Nashville, owned by Valerie, another of our mutual friends. I asked her if she'd heard about Brandon. She hadn't.

I mentioned that I had reached out to Brandon and that I was going to call my friend Dr. Moses, a respected physician at Vanderbilt Hospital, to see if they could get Brandon in to see one of their specialists as soon as possible. Frankly, I had been so consumed by my sadness that I was happy to have the chance to do something helpful for someone I loved.

The next day I received an e-mail from Brandon addressed to Valerie and to me. Valerie had contacted him and asked him what was going on with his health. He said that if he wanted his private information out in public, he would send out a press release. I explained that I had only wanted to offer to try to get him into Vanderbilt Hospital. He wrote that he had already undergone intensive testing, that the Mayo Clinic was studying the results, and that he'd know what treatment plans were available to him when the results came back. His e-mails were rude, snide, and completely out of line.

I was in an emotional black hole and wasn't spending any time with my friends anyway, so I retreated to my solitude. A few months after the e-mail exchange I heard that Brandon's grandmother had passed away. I sent flowers to her funeral. He thanked me and told me how much that had meant to him. I told him that no matter what we might have gone through or what we might go through, I loved him. And that was true.

A week or so later, I was told by a mutual friend that when

Brandon was asked if he and I had "made up," he said, "That bitch is trying to be my friend again." I'm guessing that he wanted our friends to think that I'd come crawling back with my tail between my legs begging for his friendship. That is a game he plays, and I had always let him play it because I was scared of him.

Shame and fear caused me to tolerate that abusive behavior. If I'd been able to be open about my sexuality and if I'd had nothing to hide, I would not have allowed him to treat me like that. I'd also been told over the years that he *had* told people that I was gay and claimed that I had confided in him about it, which was not true. I was a good friend to him even though he wasn't always good to me.

Now I value myself far too much to share my life with anyone other than ethical, honest, and kind people—who cherish me and let me cherish them.

One of My Angels

In late 2006, after nine months of my producer and friend Rodney Crowell's hearing my songs in their barest form as I was writing them, he called to invite me to dinner. We went to a restaurant in East Nashville. We'd barely been seated when he said, "Chely, I'm emotionally invested in these songs of yours. You need to make your record, and you need to let me help

My shepherd—Rodney Crowell—and me. 2007. (Tiffany Scott)

you." I was so broken at the time that I hadn't even entertained the thought of beginning a record. I was without a record label then, and Rodney asked if I had the money to make an album. I said I did. He explained that we would put every dime that I wanted to spend into the record and that he wanted nothing for it.

I stared at my plate and then asked him why he, one of the most respected singer/songwriter/producers of modern music, would be willing to do that for me. He smiled, with an appropriate amount of sympathy, and said that it was rare to stumble upon an artist "really going through a creative change and not afraid to give in to it."

Before Rodney and I parted ways that night, I told him that I wasn't ready to begin recording—the songs were still coming to me. He assured me that we wouldn't start recording my album until the time was right.

I thanked him for dinner—for everything—and said good night to my newfound shepherd.

The album Rodney and I started the following summer happened the way that I'd always imagined records were made—with true inspiration and what would come to be an honest heart.

A Million to One

W hen I was in second grade, my elementary school started a project that would take almost an entire school year to complete. There had been discussion among some of the students about the number 1,000,000. None of us were really able to conceptualize how big that number was, and we struggled to imagine what a million of anything looked like. Our teachers decided that we should actually see 1,000,000 of something to understand the meaning. We, the students, were going to collect one million pull tabs—the disposable pieces of metal that used to be on the top of soda cans. The new stay-on-the-can pull tabs were already in use, but our small community was littered with the throwaway kind, a danger to the naked feet of children in rural Kansas. By collecting them, we'd be doing a good thing for the safety of the barefoot population of Wellsville (which was considerable), and we'd also get a math lesson.

Each day we delivered our bounty and counted the contributions. We competed to see whose class could gather the most, and a tally was kept every day. Once we filled our Folgers coffee cans, Ziploc sandwich bags, brown paper sacks, lunch boxes, and often our pockets with those little razor-sharp treasures, we'd make our way to the grade school gymnasium to deposit them in the designated corner. Before long, our pile reached gargantuan proportions. We all marveled at the size of it. One million was *big*.

My entire life since then, when I've considered a million of anything, whether it be dollars, miles, or fans, I've always thought of that pile of aluminum pull tabs.

I've never been certain how many people are actual fans of mine, but I have it set in my head that I have one million fans. Not two million, not seventy-five thousand, but one million. I allow myself this estimation based on a couple of things that I know: I have sold a million records and I have played live concerts for at least a million people.

There was a time in my career, until recently, that I was fixated on maintaining the approval of all of these one million people. For instance, I don't eat food from McDonald's. A commercial music artist is taught not to make divisive public statements about any one group or establishment, especially a corporate entity that might be a potential sponsor. McDonald's could likely be the favorite restaurant, or perhaps the employer, of some of my fans.

My policy was that if something I might do or say were to put off just one of my one million fans, I wouldn't take that risk. I believed that I had it in my power to maintain the approval of all one million people, and anything short of pleasing every single one of them was unacceptable to me. I was afraid to let anyone down.

I knew that if my fans found out that I was gay, I'd certainly disappoint a good number of them.

As I thought about how I'd been trying to win the approval of one million fans for more than a decade, a new truth slowly and powerfully became obvious to me. I had deprived myself of a basic human need—love. That deprivation caused emotional, physical, and spiritual damage. Had I allowed it to go on, it would have killed me for sure.

I finally realized that the one million mark that I had set was not a need at all but a want. During those very pivotal months of solitude and sadness, my system of measurement was slowly, systematically, reset. Material things, which I had worked so hard to acquire, were of little or no importance to me anymore. I'd never been hung up on money or things, but I'd always understood that I couldn't live on dreams alone. I'd been frugal in my spending and aggressive in my saving. I didn't have my eye set on money so that I could buy cars, jewelry, and lavish things—that's never been my style. My objective was to save and invest every dime I made.

I started buying real estate and stocks in my early twenties. I watched my contemporaries in country music blowing through their newfound wealth, but I knew better. I anticipated that my moneymaking opportunities could, at any time, come to a screeching halt if it were ever revealed that I was gay. So I buckled down even more than a typical former low-income, blue-collar farm girl from Kansas might have.

When I found myself in the midst of my breakdown, I was surprised to realize that my financial security, which I once held in such high regard, meant absolutely nothing to me anymore. It didn't matter to me in the least when I was balled up in my bed crying that I owned real estate, had fruitful investments, and enjoyed a diversified portfolio.

I began to realize that I would have been a happier person had I lived paycheck to paycheck in a tiny apartment with my dogs and my female partner, for all the world to see. For years, the thought of that had scared me, but as I began to fully take in my sad existence—and as I discovered how hard I'd worked to achieve a high mark that provided no consolation whatsoever—living an open life as a gay woman, no matter what the consequences, didn't sound like such a bad idea.

Had I been forthcoming about my sexuality in Music City in the summer of 1989, I would never have had the opportunity to make an album—not to mention seven of them. Many who are not in my industry might suggest that I was just being paranoid and that it probably would've been okay for me to be an "out" gay country singer. To those who make that suggestion, I say, You are wrong. In a perfect world, that would have been an acceptable situation, but we do not live in a perfect world. I loved country music so much that I was not willing to compromise my chances at getting a fair shot at making records.

In my early years in Nashville, I was helped by many singers and songwriters who preached that success as an entertainer hinged on the ability to bend where you are able and willing to do so. They explained that to be a successful recording artist, you might sometimes have to do things that you'd rather not do—record a song that you don't really love, appear in a video that you think is silly, or tour with an artist whose music you can't stand. I guess I overestimated my ability to bend when it came to denying myself the freedoms of love and companionship the way that straight people were able to enjoy them. I did it for a long time, and I believed I could pull it off. But like a concrete bridge that collapses, I too crumbled. It's not as if one day that bridge's integrity was damaged and it just fell. It would have taken time for stress and bad design to catch up with it, but eventually it would finally collapse. That's what happened to me. I was no longer able to sway and bend, and I finally broke.

Rock bottom. When a person gets to the lowest of lows, faces ultimate devastation, and he or she is forced to make changes in order to survive—this is called hitting rock bottom. I had hit mine and it was clear in every part of me.

I became aware of the distinction between my wants and my needs. I wanted one million people to love, accept, and approve of me. My need was another story.

Rodney Crowell called me early one day from the airport in Los Angeles and told me that as soon as he landed in Nashville that evening he needed to come talk to me. I said okay.

He told me that since he and I had begun working together,

whenever he'd bump into music industry people in Nashville somebody would ask, "Hey, aren't you working with Chely Wright?" He'd tell them yes, and often they'd say things like "She's great," "I really like her; she's talented and a hard worker," or "She's so nice and pretty." Then Rodney told me that usually, after people complimented me, they'd ask him in a quieter voice, "Isn't Chely gay, though?"

After Rodney arrived back in Nashville, we sat on the front porch of my house and he confessed his self-proclaimed crime of betraying me. Something moved inside my chest. He asked for me to hear him out—he needed to apologize for gossiping about my sexuality.

On Rodney's flight out to Los Angeles a few days earlier, he sat next to a woman who is married to someone who used to work for me, and she asked him "the question." He said that her position was one of admiration and respect for me and that she encouraged Rodney to encourage me to be *the one* to step forward and come out of the closet. She insisted that I would be able to be a great example for the gay community because I was a respected and well-loved part of Nashville's music community. Rodney told me that because she was so sincere, he got caught up in the speculation and discussion of my personal life, even though he and I had never discussed it. He regretted his participation in it because it was not respectful of our friendship.

I shook my head with understanding and compassion as his words spilled out, and although I just wanted that conversation to end and to never discuss it again, I let him say what he needed to say. My guess was that he anticipated I'd crumble into some admission. I didn't. I had kept my secret so locked up for so long that even if I'd felt moved to share it with him then, I didn't know how.

I should have been able to tell Rodney, at that very moment, that I was gay. I was happy, relieved, and thankful to hear him tell me how much he loved me. I wanted to break through that wall of secrecy and be folded into his arms of acceptance, friendship, and love. Instead, I stayed behind the wall I'd spent the better part of thirty years constructing, maintaining, and fortifying.

After Rodney had purged himself of what he called his betrayal of me, I thanked him for loving me enough to confess something to me that I surely would never have found out. He knew that too, I suppose, but for him it wasn't about that. He didn't tell me because he thought he'd get caught gossiping about me. He told me because that's the kind of person he is—honorable.

For so many years, I'd pinned myself down in front of the jury of one million. My jury was a collection of strangers, yet I allowed them to sit in judgment of me. Beautifully, and just in time, I found myself sitting face-to-face with one friend. I knew his heart and he knew mine.

The recalibration of my brain, my body, and my soul during those painful months made itself known. I had gone from wanting one million to accept me to needing just one. A million to one—that's a long way to travel, but I thank God I made the journey.

Choice

In 1999 I stopped eating red meat, poultry, and pork. I still eat dairy products and eggs, so this technically makes me an ovo-lacto-vegetarian. In terms of making things simpler to explain to most people, I call myself a vegetarian.

I have a friend named Susan, back in Nashville, who is a Harley Girl. She and her husband ride the big, hard-to-miss motorcycles every chance they get. She doesn't just ride on the back of her husband's bike—she has a bike of her own. They spend their weekends on their motorcycles and take vacations with other Harley lovers. Susan has a couple of tattoos, some body piercing, and leather clothing; Susan is an authentic Harley Girl.

I have another friend, named Garland, who is a gym rat. He hits the gym at least five days a week, and I'm convinced that if he could go without actually having to hold down a job he'd spend twelve hours a day in the gym. The only socializing he does is with his fellow fitness fiends; even when Garland is not doing cardio or pumping iron, he's thinking about it. He abides by his self-governed diet, which dictates, according to his regimented exercise routine, exactly what to eat and when to eat it. Carbohydrates are allowed at a certain time, fats at another; he's got to meet the mandated quota for grams of protein before the clock strikes a certain hour or he'll turn into a pumpkin or worse.

Vegetarian, Harley Girl, gym rat. These are lifestyles, and they're chosen.

Homosexuality is not a lifestyle. It is not chosen. One doesn't have the choice to be white, black, Asian, tall, or Native American, and I did not choose to be gay.

Components of choice actually do exist in my story, but there is a critical delineation that must be noted. The only true choices in my story are that I chose to hide and now I'm choosing to stop lying to myself and to the rest of the world. My plans for a normal and happy life never stood a chance when I was choosing to hide. I was trying to construct a house on a faulty foundation, and although I did my best to make it beautiful and pleasing to everyone who might see, my impressive structure was built on sand, on lies.

Like most gay people I know, I watch television, listen to the radio, and scour the Internet in disbelief as the conservative right spews the inaccuracy that being gay is a choice. Many of these groups, guided by uninformed leadership, believe that one can "pray the gay away." One cannot. There are some documentary films about the ex-gay philosophy and the process of becoming straight. There are personal testimonials from people who claim that they were able to become straight, but when the filmmakers followed up with them years later most admitted that they are still gay and always will be.

These people endured incredible pressure from their families, instructors, and church leaders to be a success story, to prove that "praying the gay away" works. Sadly, whether or not they are "able" to stop being gay gets attached to their faith in God, and they find themselves in double jeopardy. If homosexuals cannot "go straight," their Christianity is then judged and graded, rendering them a failure in their sexuality and a failure in their faith. Many later claim that while going through the classes to become straight, they made a choice not to act on their homosexual instincts, even though they knew that they were still gay.

There's that word again: "choice." One can choose not to act on one's homosexual nature—for a while, but that choice will take its toll mentally, spiritually, possibly even physically, as it did with me.

Stereotypes

The first person identified as a homosexual to me was Billie Jean King. I was about nine years old. My mother and I were watching a weekend sporting event on television, and Billie Jean King was on camera, doing commentary on a tennis match. It took me a second to determine her gender. I asked my mom why that lady was dressed like a man. "Because she's gay." She said it without a vocal inflection that leaned toward the negative or the positive, but her answer introduced a stereotype to my young mind. If a woman dresses "like that," she's a homosexual. Nevertheless, on that day, my mom went on to tell me what a pioneer Billie Jean King was in her sport and that she could beat the boys at tennis.

I asked myself, "That's what gay looks like?" My confusion and isolation escalated, leaving me just one image of a gay woman to fixate on for a long time. The next homosexual I learned about was Martina Navratilova, a couple of years after I saw Billie Jean King on our television set. I didn't dress like them—pants suits and collared shirts—and I didn't have my hair cut short like they did, but I wondered if I would eventually grow up to look like them. I was afraid that the way they appeared was the way that I was destined to become. It scared me because I couldn't imagine how a woman who had an appear-

*I knew from a young age that part of being a
woman in country music meant sparkly clothes
and lots of hair and makeup. One of my favorite
photographers, Sheryl Nields, took this for*
Country Weekly. *2002.*

ance like they did would ever be able to sing on the stage of the
Grand Ole Opry. All of the female country music singers I'd
seen on television or in pictures were in frilly dresses with
sequins and had long, flowing hair. At that young age, I was very
discouraged about all of it.

As I look back on my years of hiding in the closet, I realize
that I was struggling with my own negative and confusing feelings about gays. I recall at times being angry and frustrated with

This photo was taken in 2002. As any woman in today's society knows, getting to the place in life where you can feel good about your body and about being sensual—well, it's a milestone. I'm very proud of this shot. (Dean Dixon)

gay women. Over the past couple of years in particular, I've come to learn that internalized homophobia is often experienced by homosexuals in hiding.

The gays that I projected negative judgment upon were the gays that couldn't hide by passing as straight and the gays who just flat out refused to hide. I did resent what I saw in these people because I felt that they were in control of the definition and description of a homosexual, and I didn't approve of the picture they were painting. I wanted them to "act normal"—to try harder to go unnoticed—and I'd think, "Why are they doing that? They're making it so hard for everyone." I wondered why the effeminate boys couldn't act a little more masculine. I wished that the not-so-femme lesbians I saw would just put on a skirt and wear a little makeup.

I see the hypocrisy in my thinking now, but it has taken me a long time to understand what exactly was going on inside me. I had never been completely and totally feminine. I was a tomboy some of the time and a feminine girl too. I felt very comfortable both ways. So why wouldn't I be more accepting and compassionate about the lesbians that I've seen in my adult life who are less than ultra-feminine? Complex, multifaceted fear is the answer to that question. I had a fear that if someone noticed a not-so-feminine behavior or characteristic in me, they would know that I was a homosexual. And in my young, frightened mind, being "found out" as a homosexual was the worst thing that could ever happen to a person. I was taught and repeatedly reminded to have this fear—by society and by my church.

Had I been around when Rosa Parks was taking her stand, I might have been harsh and frustrated with her too. I would probably have suggested to her that she was causing an unnecessary scene and that she should just make things easier by sitting in the back of the bus. Why cause a stir, Rosa? Why do you have to draw attention to yourself, Rosa? You're making things difficult for everyone, Rosa. Stop pushing the situation to a boiling point. So those gays who couldn't hide or wouldn't hide were essentially holding a mirror up to my face and reminding me that because I could hide and I did, I was a coward. And I was.

The more I read about other people's coming-out process and the more conversations I have had with other homosexuals to whom I've reached out, the more I understand that my disdain for certain behaviors and images of gays is directly related to my own self-acceptance. Somehow I have to be able to rid myself of the negative stereotypes and the stigma of homosexuality. Even though I have known my whole life that I am gay and that there is nothing that I can do to change it, the fact still remains that I was taught that it is wrong, and my sensibilities have held on to those prejudices for more than thirty years.

Perhaps I *could* have hidden my homosexuality for the rest of my life, but that's not how I want to live. Shedding more light on the argument that no one can say definitively what gay "looks like" does play into my decision to step forward, but it is not my most powerful motivation for coming out. I am standing up for myself, because if I don't, I will never be whole. That my story might help others find comfort, safety, and understanding is a beautiful by-product of truth.

My Mom, My Brother, and Others

I love my mom, and I want to be closer to her. I am not ready to tell her that I am gay, but when I do I hope that she will accept me and love me. If she doesn't, it will hurt, but I will find a way to survive it.

I told my brother, Chris, that I was gay during a phone conversation in 2006. He was going through a stressful time with his family. He had called me in a panic to tell me that at the age of thirty-eight he was going to be a grandpa.

His seventeen-year-old daughter had unexpectedly gotten pregnant. I did my best to be a voice of reason, telling him that this wasn't the time to be angry with her and that the most important thing to focus on was that a baby was on the way. He was disappointed in her for being irresponsible and for lying to him about doing things she swore she wasn't doing.

I encouraged him to think about the present and not get hung up on the recent past that landed her in such a precarious situation. I also told him that a lot of teenagers are sexually active, like it or not, and that most teenagers who are lie to their parents about it.

"Well, you didn't do it," he said. "You didn't get pregnant. You were a good girl." I recall thinking that I really didn't want to tell my brother at that moment my deepest secret, but I felt that in doing so, I might offer some balance and objectivity to the conversation. I said, "Chris, you're right—I didn't have sex in high school. I hate to break this to you right now on the phone, but the reason I didn't have sex in high school probably has a lot to do with the fact that I am gay. It was not difficult for me to resist having sex with boys. I was a good girl, yes, but having sex and getting pregnant was never a worry for me."

He barely acknowledged what I'd told him. He just said, "Really? I didn't know that." He said he needed to get back to work and got off the phone. He didn't say that he'd call me back or that he wanted to talk to me about this at another time. I spent the next day feeling scared and anxious about it, and I called him. He didn't pick up the phone, and I left a voice mail asking him not to mention what I'd shared with him to anyone. He never called back to assure me that my secret was safe with him, to tell me that he loved me no matter what, or even to ask questions about my life.

For most of Chris's career in the Marine Corps, my being his sister has been a source of pride and joy to him. Even though it bothers him when other Marines make comments about his sister being pretty, he has always been proud of being my brother.

I know that Chris is proud of me and of the good things I have done with my life, but I'm not sure what his feelings are about my being gay. It seems a brother and sister who've grown up together, liking, respecting, and loving each other, should have an easier time discussing something like this.

For years I forfeited being with my partner during holidays because I wanted to be with my brother and his family, and I was put in a position of having to choose. Often I'd finish my tour a few days before Thanksgiving or Christmas, get off my tour bus in Nashville, pack another suitcase, and fly to where Chris and his family were stationed at the time. I was viewed as the sister who had no life outside of her career and nowhere else to be.

I couldn't really say, "Hey, I think I'll head out your way the day after Christmas because I want to spend Christmas Day with my partner." I was no different from my siblings—I had a partner too. We had a home together, and she had a family that we would have liked to have visited.

I was hurt that Chris never acknowledged that I had shown up for my family even though I had other choices of how to spend my time—and what that must've been like for me.

For more than three years after I told Chris that I was gay, we carried on as if nothing had happened, talking on the phone occasionally (albeit less frequently than usual, which made me feel a little rejected). He wouldn't ask me how I was, and I would mostly inquire about him and ask how his family was.

Recently I called my brother, thinking I would get his voice-mail, and instead he picked up. We each gave our usual friendly greeting, and then I cut to the point.

I was calling to ask him if he'd consider being interviewed for a documentary being made about my coming out.

"Chris, the filmmakers want to know if you'd be willing to sit down and talk to them on camera. I was sure you'd say no, but I figured I'd better let you make that decision. I love you, and I care about what you have to say. But if you don't want to, that's okay too."

"Well, it depends on what you want me to say."

"I want you to be honest," I said to him. "And if they ask you something you don't want to answer, you don't have to answer."

I was on Lexington Avenue in New York City. The traffic was loud as it rumbled by me. I had the cell phone pressed tightly to my ear and was just steps from the train. I was just about to tell Chris I'd have to call him later, and we could discuss it then.

"Sis," Chris said, "I don't think you know how much I love you and support you."

My eyes filled up with tears. It was the first time he had said anything like that to me since I'd told him I was gay. Chris is a Master Sergeant in the Marines, and he is tough as nails. He had always been unable to go beyond our customary telephone salutation of "I love you too." This discussion about my homosexuality—and his declaration of his love and support for me—was different. Hearing my brother say those words made me feel happy and hopeful.

"Wow, Chris, that makes me cry. I didn't know."

"Have them call me," he said. "I'd love to be involved."

We both said good-bye and hung up.

Where Do I Fit In?

I'm willing to fight for myself and to live an honest and fully realized life, but I still have a lot to learn. Trying to find my place in the gay community is enough to make my head spin at times.

I had heard about Gay Pride events for years from my gay friends. They'd told me how magical it was to be surrounded by hundreds of thousands of people who are different, like you.

On June 30, 2008, I attended the Gay Pride Parade in New York City. My friends were excited to show me around for the first time. We left my apartment in Chelsea and headed downtown to Fifteenth and Fifth to another friend's apartment.

A block away from our first glimpse of the parade I couldn't believe the rumble and the roar I was hearing. I'm no stranger to large gatherings of people, but for some reason I was shocked at the thousands of people lining the streets on both sides up and down Fifth Avenue—people of all ages and of every ethnicity imaginable. For the first thirty minutes or so, as we stood on the sidewalk doing our best to peek around the shoulders and heads in front of us, I saw marchers and floats. Most of the floats were clearly marked, identifying their group, and I was astonished that all of these people had somehow found one another and decided to make a float.

I saw BUTCH LESBIANS written on a sign, and sure enough, about fifty women fitting that description walked together with a purpose and with visible comfort. There was an ornate and colorful float announcing the "Drag Queens of Detroit." There were scores of musicians playing at high volume strategically placed in the parade so that when the sounds of one group would start to fade, those of another would become audible.

I had wondered the night before the parade and all day leading up to it if I would be emotionally moved by what I would see. In the first half hour of the parade, although it was entertaining and exciting to see, it wasn't an emotional experience for me. Then Chuck nudged my elbow and said, "Here comes the PFLAG* float." I stretched my neck as far as I could and saw about a hundred people walking arm in arm. They had signs written on poster board and stapled to tall wooden slats, T-shirts with individual messages stenciled across them, and even a few signs with no wooden post or poll.

Some marching in the PFLAG group held both arms up over their heads, hoisting their signs with overwhelming commitment. As I read the words of their signs, I began to cry. PFLAG: WE LOVE OUR CHILDREN JUST AS THEY ARE. MY DAUGHTER IS A LESBIAN AND SHE IS TEACHING ME ABOUT LOVE. THERE IS NOTHING WRONG WITH MY SON. As I read the heartfelt messages, I thought about my dad and wondered if he would walk out in that street for me. I thought about my aunt Char and how, shortly after I came out to her, she asked me what books she should purchase. I thought about my mother, in whom I hadn't confided, and wondered if I would ever see her holding a sign for me.

As I watched the parade, I searched and searched for the group where I'd fit in, but I never saw my group. I fast-forwarded to next year's Gay Pride event and tried to imagine

*Parents, Families, and Friends of Lesbians and Gays

myself marching in the parade. What would my float say? GAY COUNTRY SINGERS?

I had this notion that if I attended this Gay Pride event I'd feel at home, like I finally belonged. But I didn't. Perhaps once I've come out, I will find my place.

Hate Crimes Are Down?

Looking back at my school days in Kansas, I can't help but wonder how much worse I would have been treated had my tormentors known I was a lesbian. I know that for many gay children and teens—especially those who cannot or don't hide their sexuality—school can be a nightmare.

When I have discussed harassment and violence against gays, I've found that many believe hate crimes to be a thing of the past. And when I hear that, I think of Matthew Shepard, who was tortured and murdered in 1998 by two young men who hated and feared him simply because of his sexuality. I think of Lawrence King, a fifteen-year-old boy murdered by a classmate in Oxnard, California, in 2008 because he made the mistake of giving his killer a Valentine's Day card.

When you grow up gay, you fear that others will strike out at you simply because of who you are. The intent behind bullying and more horrifying acts of violence against gays is the same: to make sure the victims know that they need to lay low, keep silent, and above all realize that they'll never be accepted because they are defective and have no place in society. For many young people, that rejection is too much to bear and they turn to suicide. Even if the hater isn't the one to swing the bat or pull the trigger, it's still a hate crime. Even if the hater gets the victim to do his dirty work by committing suicide, it's murder just the same.

When a gay child commits suicide because society cannot bear his existence, I believe it is a hate crime.

When a gay teenager slips into depression or drug addiction because she has been conditioned to hate herself, who's to blame? She grows tired of trying to numb herself with drugs and alcohol, and she knows that she's never going to be able to change the fact that she's gay—so she takes her own life. Then when people hear about her death, will they say, "Oh, she was a mess. She was strung out on drugs. She was a real screwup"? We may not hear about it as the top story on the six o'clock news, that another hate crime against a homosexual has taken place, but it has and it does.

I don't like bullies. I never have. It hurts me when I'm picked on, and when I see others being picked on, it stirs a lot of emotion in me. It's not funny or clever to pick on someone—it is mean and it's wrong.

I got picked on at different times in school for many reasons. My sister was picked on because she was overweight; my brother was bullied because he was not quick to swing a fist—we were all made to feel like we didn't belong.

Exclusion from others causes pain, and it can be as dangerous and damaging to a person as getting a bullet in the heart or being shoved headfirst into a toilet in the locker room while the attackers laugh and slap high fives. "You're not one of us. You don't belong. We don't like you. You're not good enough. There is something wrong with you, and there is nothing wrong with us."

That feeling I had in fourth grade when Mrs. Lawyer encouraged me to do the right thing—to defend the innocent—hasn't faded much. I felt a relief when I sat on those stairs with Mrs. Lawyer and told the truth in the name of justice.

I feel a familiar relief about coming out and telling my story.

Turning the Page

Moving to New York was a big change for me. It is a place where I can be myself—eventually. This city is one of the most diverse places on earth, and it is much easier to blend in here than anywhere I've ever lived. That being said, I haven't quite turned the page. I'm not living openly as a gay woman here yet.

I've never really had the opportunity to date women. I have a close friend who suggested that since I could blend in here, I should go to a lesbian bar. Although I do get recognized in New York on occasion, I was confident that I could go to a lesbian bar and not be noticed.

The week I moved here, my sister, Jeny, was with me, and we took a break from painting and cleaning my new apartment to have a little fun. We met up with Chuck and we went to have a drink at a lesbian bar in the Village, just to see what it was like.

We sat in the back corner observing the women in the bar. A jukebox hanging on the wall displayed a photograph of the artists as their music was played. Chuck went over to see what kind of music was available. A minute or so later, he walked back to our table and said, "Chels, they've got all of your records on the jukebox." As he sat down, one of my songs, "Jezebel," began to play.

As soon as it started, several of the twenty girls in the bar shouted out, "Yeah! I love this song!" and started to move in their seats. They knew the song and they knew me. I got up and walked out the door. Jeny and Chuck didn't understand why I got anxious. I tried to explain to them that being in a lesbian bar and being recognized was not funny to me. It's going to take some time for me to feel comfortable in my new life.

I'm not suggesting that everyone in Nashville will be shocked to know the truth about my sexuality, but they'll probably be shocked that I'm telling the world.

After I come out, there will be no shortage of people who will say, "Oh, I knew that. People have said that about Chely for years. We all knew that." I can assure you that *thinking* and *knowing* are two different things. And telling the world is in a league of its own.

As I have mentioned several times in this book, a compelling motivation for me to come forward is to comfort young people as they come to realize and deal with the fact that they are gay.

If that's you, hear my story. I want you to know that you are not sick and you are not alone.

I look forward to speaking to young people—gay and straight—to their parents and their loved ones to help further understanding of what it's like to face a society that largely condemns homosexuality.

There are still horrific acts of violence being perpetrated against gay people, and those atrocities should be a wake-up call to those who feel unsympathetic or disconnected to the suffering of any minority group. Our society simply cannot allow ignorance and hate to be acted upon. Physical, emotional, social, and religious crimes are committed against minorities every single day—at work, at school, while trying to hail a cab, or while walking down the street. You may think that you're not a minority so you don't have to worry. You might want to think about that again with a bit more examination. Are you, in any way, a minority? And if you think you're not, you're lucky. If that's you, what will you say to those of us who are minorities and need an ally? Will you turn away or will you stand up for someone in need?

I hear the word "tolerance"—that some people are trying to teach people to be tolerant of gays. I'm not satisfied with that word. I am gay, and I am not seeking to be "tolerated." One tolerates a toothache, rush-hour traffic, an annoying neighbor with a cluttered yard. I am not a negative to be tolerated, and I don't think that other minority groups would feel comforted and equal to hear leaders of the general public self-righteously proclaim that "we" should "tolerate them." That's not equality.

I have noticed that when other well-known people in entertainment come out of the closet, they do sometimes enjoy a certain overwhelming acceptance. I think it's good when those who have come out say in interviews that they can't believe how much support they have received from their peers, from the press, and from their fans. I have no doubt that the support is real, but I can't help but think of the people they didn't hear from.

For the most part, I believe that those who don't approve are less likely to come forward and say so. Perhaps it's the private, secret disdain and hatred that are the most dangerous. Generations of clandestine haters have done their most effective work cloaked in white sheets, without a single public statement—

allowing them to remain nameless and faceless. That's what scares me the most.

I consider myself lucky to have people in my life who have accepted me and cradled me in support. My dad's response upon learning that I was gay was shocking and inspiring to me. I'm not saying that he understands it or that he is "cool" with it, but every time we talk he makes sure to tell me that he is proud of me and that this experience has forced him to think.

Not too long ago he told me that he thought he knew what "gay" was and that it represented sinfulness, deviance, promiscuity, and a lack of goodness. After I came out to him in that Midwestern hotel room, he had to reconsider what "gay" is; he knew that I didn't fit into his old definition of the word. I am proud of my dad, and I am thankful for him.

Since my aunt Char and my sister, Jeny, found out, they have each sought education about homosexuality through books, articles, and documentary films. I don't tell them what to believe and what not to believe. I simply encourage them to continue listening and to use their hearts and their minds. Their love and support mean everything to me.

Learning to Say Good-bye

It would be wrong to blame my breakup with Julia on John Rich—he was merely the catalyst. The real killer was my hiding.

I have never loved anyone the way I loved Julia. Even writing her name causes old feelings to be stirred up. I ask myself if things would have been different had I been able to stand up and openly declare my love for her. But I didn't stand up. Too much was at stake, and I lost the only thing that mattered to me.

I still dream of Julia—dreams that feel so real, that's what makes them so painful.

I see us walking in Radnor Park in the fall. We're side by side as we walk through the blanket of gold- and rust-colored leaves. Occasionally I have to adjust my step to slow down for her, because my legs are longer than hers. Walking together was something we became good at over the years, and it was as much a part of our being a couple as finishing one another's sentences or making love—moving together along paths, sidewalks, and trails as one. I knew her stride and she knew mine.

In the dream, we're walking. I look over and see her profile, the familiar lines of her chin and her nose, the way her bangs brush her brow, and I think to myself that she's even prettier than the day I met her. She became more attractive to me as the years went by, and when I see her in my sleep, she's beautiful.

In February 2002 I gave Julia a ring. I'd given her jewelry before, but this ring signified something more; it meant forever. She and I had been through the toughest of times, and even though I didn't know exactly how we would manage the complexities of staying together while continuing to hide in the closet, I knew that I couldn't stand the thought of being without her. As I shopped for months to find the perfect ring, I spent a lot of time thinking about what that ring would mean to us.

I was nervous about taking the step, but I assumed that uncertainty and anxiety were likely the same in heterosexual couples at the crossroads of commitment. I relaxed and went with my heart.

It was Valentine's Day and we were upstairs on the floor of the guest bedroom, playing with our dogs, as we did most evenings after we got home from our workdays. The bedroom was carpeted, and the dogs preferred playing up there because they could get traction to run. Knowing that we'd end up in that spot, I had placed the gift-wrapped ring in the top drawer of the bedside nightstand.

My insides were shaking, and just when I couldn't take it any longer, I said, "Close your eyes." She resisted and asked why—reminding me that our date the night before had been our Valentine's Day gift to each other and that if I'd gone ahead and gotten her a gift, she was going to feel bad because she had stuck to our pact and didn't buy me one. I convinced her to close her eyes, and I gently put the small silver box with the little red bow in the palm of her hand. She opened her eyes and knew instantly what I had done. Perhaps she flashed back to the months before, to the times I had steered her by a few jewelry stores and casually taken note of what she liked and didn't like.

Julia slowly peeled the paper off the box, took the smaller blue box in her hands, and opened the lid. "I love it," she said. She put it on her finger and extended her arm out in front of her, tipped her head to one side, squinted her eyes ever so slightly, admired her gift, and smiled. Then I handed her the card that I had carefully chosen, and she read what I'd written inside.

She cried. I cried. We hugged and kissed while our dogs brought us squeaky toys and multicolored ropes. Had it been legal for us to marry, and had I not been a well-known person in country music, I would have asked her to marry me—and I think she would've said yes.

Recently I had a dream about that night, and the details were just as I'd described. It would've been easier had the dream not seemed so real, had I realized midway through that it didn't make sense and that it was just a dream. Instead, I woke up to an alarm clock and the realization that Julia and I were not together.

I regret that I gave in to fear and selfishness and chose to leave Julia. I regret that when we had the chance to reconcile in 2006, I was not ready to stand up and speak the truth—even though I had had a frightening glance into how unhappy my life could be without real love. Even then I was too scared. I regret that I put others' opinions of me before me and the woman I loved. I regret that I didn't have enough self-confidence to choose a partner who wanted me to be happy in my life, career included. I regret that Julia's biggest fear and accusation of me for so many years came true. She used to tell me that she was afraid I cared more about my career and my image than I did about her. I regret that I proved her right.

I have oceans of regret. I have found a positive direction in my life, a true north. I feel lucky to have such deep waters beneath me, because every drop is a reminder to me of the power of truth, and all of those drops combined can deliver me to new places.

I have forgiven myself for my mistakes. Now I know that nothing is more important than my health, my happiness, and my heart.

State of the Union

I moved to New York City in June 2008. As I write my story, I am filled with excitement, fear, anxiety, and glimmers of liberation and hope. I am trying to prepare myself. A few of my friends might be angry with me for not trusting them enough to confide in them, but I just hope that once they've read my story they'll understand why I handled it the way I did. Many people that I've employed over the years are conservative Christians, and to them homosexuality is nothing more than a deviant, sinful choice that some recklessly make, putting their salvation at risk. During my career, I have sat in the front lounge of my tour bus or around dinner tables with my employees as some of them have quoted scripture and pontificated about the sins of homosexuality to anyone who would listen.

It was never pointed at me specifically, because I was good at hiding, but the condemnation, ignorance, and judgment left me frustrated and angry.

I have lived with a great deal of shame in allowing that kind of discussion to happen in my presence, and I'm trying to forgive myself for it. It's not that I didn't raise questions to their small-minded arguments. I did. But I didn't want to invite speculation about my sexuality. I sat through those discussions because I genuinely wanted to hear their opinions. I truly do believe in everyone's right to their own beliefs.

I realize that this will be far more difficult than I imagine—it already has been.

I cry most days as I write this down. I'm uncovering a lifetime of imposed shame and fear. I'm happy to be telling my story because it makes me feel whole for the first time in my life.

In addition to my everyday life of writing and recording, I spend time thinking about what it will be like when I do step forward. Can I help people understand what it's like to be gay? Will I be able to further identify homosexuality and some of the inherent challenges that we face? I am focused on being ready— I feel like an athlete in training.

I told a couple of my friends who already knew my secret that I was going to come out of the closet. I realized that I would have to let a few more people into my life and into my business to help me through the process.

I've zigzagged across the nation, from Nashville to New York City, Atlanta to Los Angeles and back, to seek out sensitive and qualified people to help me come out of hiding. I had to come out to every one of those people that I went to see, and anyone who's ever come out before can tell you it's exhausting. I've sat with no fewer than thirty people and shared my story to help them gain a full understanding of how my life in hiding has been.

I've been nervous since the day I decided to do this. One can ask people to keep one's secret, but sometimes they don't. I've known this my entire career, and it's exactly why I seldom confided in anyone.

If you were to ask a fan why they love country singers, their answer would likely be "Because they are so real." Every time I heard a fan say that about me—and I did so often—it made me sick to my stomach. I was hiding a big part of myself from my fans, and I feared that most of them would not understand or approve of who I really was.

I have no idea if or how many of my fans will support me in my journey from this point forward, and I have no idea where I might find my audience.

I am a musician and a songwriter. I have dedicated my life to performing for an audience, and my work has paid off. I don't know what will happen, but I am at peace with the uncertainty of it all.

ACKNOWLEDGMENTS

I would like to acknowledge a collection of souls who assisted and accompanied me during the creation of this book. Thank you:

Russell Carter, my manager—for your abundant gifts of mind and spirit and the demeanor with which you impart them. I am so grateful for you.

Sonny Mehta—for your invaluable help; and to Gary Fisketjon—for weighing in on respect and reason.

Victoria Wilson, my editor—for editing my book.

Luke Janklow—for getting my book to Random House.

Claire Dipple—for explaining the earliest stages and for the encouragement.

Carmen Johnson—for being so efficient, so helpful, and so pleasant.

Brian Loucks—for being the first of many dots and for connecting me to dot number two.

Rodney Crowell, my shepherd—for appearing as my teacher the moment I was ready to learn.

Mitchell Gold—for writing the book *Crisis* and for being my mentor and friend.

Steve Buckingham—for your loyal friendship.

Thank you, Kevin Welk, Gary Paczosa, Bobbie Berleffi, Beverly Kopf, Tim Schofield, Howard Bragman, Bill Kapfer, Eric Baker, Neil Guiliano, Diana Rodreguiz, Eliza Byard, Reverednd Welton Gaddy, Bishop Gene Robinson, and Robert V. Taylor.

. . .

And on an even more personal note:

Chuck Walter—for being a shining example of truth and peace and for wanting me, above all things, to be happy.

Claudia Crowell—for your serene support and your unwavering compassion.

Jan Volz—for everything. I do not know a better man. With you, I have learned what real friendship is about.

Mich McCready—for who you are and for being my family.

Mary Karr—for your friendship, for the Sunday dinners, for empowering me, and for showing me the ropes.

Ashen Keilyn—for being my friend.

Anne Marie and Jeff Davidson—for the love.

Joe Tam—for your sweet heart.

John and Joy Day—for support.

Mike Vaden—for fifteen years of trust.

To my family:

My dad, Stan—for loving me "because."

My mom, Cheri—for always telling me I was special and for showing me how to beat the odds.

To my aunt Char—for being a constant in my life and for rolling up your sleeves.

To my brother, Chris—for being you, tough on the outside and tender on the inside.

To my sister, Jeny (Jennifer)—for being my best friend for a lifetime and a true inspiration.

xo chely